The Art of CHRISTMAS CRAFTS

The Art of
CHRISTMAS
CRAFTS

a Salamander book

Published by Salamander Books Limited
LONDON

Published by Salamander Books Ltd.,
129-137 York Way,
London N7 9LG,
United Kingdom

ISBN 0 86101 780 3

CREDITS

Contributors: Rosalind Burdett, Jan Hall, Karen Lansdown, Suzie Major, Susy Smith and Sarah Waterkeyn

Editor: Jilly Glassborow

Designers: Kathy Gummer, Barry Savage and Tony Truscott

Photographers: Terry Dilliway and Steve Tanner

Typeset by: Barbican Print and Marketing Services, London, and The Old Mill, London

Colour Separation by: Fotographics Ltd., London – Hong Kong, and Scantrans Pte Ltd., Singapore

Printed in Italy

CONTENTS

INTRODUCTION

It's that time of year again when our thoughts turn to parties and presents, when we bedeck our homes with paper chains, tinsel and holly, and wear funny hats at table. And what better way to get into the spirit of Christmas than to make your own decorations — hours of fun for all the family and so much cheaper than buying them.

With fully illustrated step-by-step instructions this colourful book will show you how to make over 150 dazzling designs. There are Christmas tree decorations, paper chains, stars, bells, baubles, garlands, greeting card trellises, and party hats and masks. And for that special festive dinner party or the big day itself there's a stunning range of designs to brighten up your table — centrepieces, napkin folds, placemats, name cards, crackers and other attractive table gifts.

Flowers are always a favourite at Christmas and, as well as featuring some colourful flesh flower displays, there's an exciting array of dried flower designs that will see you through the whole festive season — and on to the next! The section on gift wrapping and greetings cards is packed with original ideas for making your own paper, tags and decorative ties and bows and also includes lots of ingenious ways to disguise gifts such as records and bottles to keep the recipient guessing.

A gift is more special if it's handmade; the 35 ideas featured in the last chapter of the book range from seasonal soft toys (a Santa Claus, a snowman and a polar bear) to floral gifts, stationery and painted china.

CHRISTMAS DECORATIONS

Of all the Christmas decorations, the Christmas tree is without doubt the most dazzling. This chapter contains a wealth of designs for decorating trees, including fake baubles, mini crackers, edible stars, sugar bells, paper lanterns and many more. Or, if you prefer a more sophisticated look, you could copy one of the stunning, though slightly more expensive, designs shown on the opening pages. The chapter also features colourful ribbon trees — a good substitute for the real thing — a host of pretty paper chains and garlands, some ingenious ways of displaying Christmas cards, lots of delightful wall hangings and a small but fun range of party hats and masks.

GO FOR GOLD

This traditional tree (right) is covered in tinsel, baubles and lametta (icicles), all in gold. A similarly elegant effect could be achieved using silver on a fake white tree; or if you have a fake silver tree, try bright pink or blue. Stick to one colour only for the most professional-looking results. If the children want to hang chocolate figures on the tree, buy some colour-coordinated ones!

Start by hanging a string of white or gold lights over the tree. Lights always make the vital difference to a Christmas tree; it is lovely to switch them on when night falls. Next, trail thick gold tinsel around the branches, concealing the light cord.

The baubles can then go on, followed by strands of lametta (icicles). At the top of the tree you could place an angel or star. The star shape shown is made from loops of tinsel — simple, but very effective. The finishing touch is a pile of gold-wrapped presents at the foot of the tree. Choose some shiny wrapping paper and cover empty boxes. If you put your presents under the tree, add a few fakes too; otherwise it looks terribly bare once the presents have been opened.

LOVELY LACE

TARTAN TIES

For a more old-fashioned look, omit sparkly baubles and lights, and stick to lace, ribbons and a few paper doilies. Start with some silk flowers wired onto the branches or simply placed on them. Take some wide lace edging and thread thin rose-coloured ribbon through the straight edge; gather it into a rosette over the ends of the branches. Allow the ends to hang down as shown.

In the gaps place some fans made from circular white paper doilies, cut in half and lightly pleated. Onto these, staple little ribbon bows, again letting the ends hang down. The pot the tree is standing in has been wrapped in plain brown paper and decorated with a large paper fan made from a rectangular doily.

Here is an unusual and very attractive way of decorating the tree. First take a set of candle lights and fasten them onto the tree. Next, you need a large bunch of gypsophilia (baby's breath). You should be able to get this even at Christmas from a good florist.

Split up the gypsophilia and simply poke it into the tree until all the gaps between branches are filled. Although bought fresh, gypsophilia should last a few days on the tree. Next you need a piece of tartan fabric, about half a metre (yard). Cut it into strips and tie them into bows on the ends of the branches. Cover the pot or stand in coloured crepe paper and tie a large bow around it.

Dried flowers always look beautiful but are especially decorative at Christmas. Brighten up the Christmas tree with sprays of dried flowers tied with tartan ribbon. Choose warm red, russet and golden yellow coloured foliage and as bright a coloured tartan as you can find so that the colours will stand out against the tree. Balance the flowers amongst the branches.

Tie a larger spray upside down at the top of the tree. Next, tie together some cinnamon sticks with tartan ribbon and hang them from the branches on fine thread. As a finishing touch, hang fir cones on narrow ribbons. Stand the tree in a basketwork pot decorated with dried flower heads glued around the rim and tartan ribbon fastened with fine wire.

This tree's stunning effect is easy to achieve. Cut star shapes from silver cardboard (see template on page 162) and position them between the branches. Then make bows from pink paper rope and place them in the gaps. The trimmings can also be hung on fine thread if the branches are rather sparse. Top the tree with a large silver star, attached with a length of wire taped to the back.

For the bows, cut a 33cm (13in) length of paper rope or use a 10cm (4in) wide crepe paper strip; bend the ends to the centre and tightly bind with sticky tape. Cut a 20cm (8in) length for the tails. Bend in half and squeeze the centre, then stick behind the bow. Bind the tails to the bow with a narrow strip and trim the tail ends diagonally. To finish, cover the tub with crepe paper.

This is especially for the kids; but be warned: you will have to exert extreme control, or the tree will be looking very bare by Boxing Day (December 26th)! On this tree we have hung iced cookies (see the instructions on page 12), little meringues and, for the grown-ups, some Amaretti biscuits — nice with the after-dinner port!

Also hung on the tree are some cute wooden cut-outs in the shape of Santa Claus, teddy bears and other favourites. You could easily make them into a mobile after Christmas, to hang in a child's bedroom. To complete the effect, some huge gingerbread men, one at the top of the tree, some in the lower branches — perhaps too well within reach of small fingers!

This is a very pretty way to treat a synthetic white tree. The lights used are large, cone-shaped white tree lights. Next, hang on lots of baubles: pastel satin, white satin with pink bows, silver with embroidered flowers.

Now simply take lengths of pastel ribbon, such as the pink, green and blue shown here, and tie them onto the ends of the branches — some in bows, the others hanging down in strands. Tie a large bow at the top of the tree. Cover the pot or stand in silver wrapping paper, and tie a large pastel bow around it.

These ornaments are very easy to make; all you need are some bells from last year's tree. If you haven't got any, look for suitable moulds in the cake decorating section of a department store. Take some ordinary granulated sugar, put a few spoonfuls in a dish, and moisten it with food colouring.

When the colouring is thoroughly mixed in, push the sugar into a bell mould, pressing it in firmly to fill the entire cavity.

Now simply tap the sugar bell out of the mould. Leave the bells to dry out overnight. To hang them on the tree, cut out a little tissue paper flower, thread a loop through it and glue it to the top of the bell. (These ornaments are not edible, and should be placed out of the reach of small children.)

Here is another cute tree decoration that is fun to make: tiny Christmas puddings. You start with ordinary ping pong balls. Spear each one onto a fine knitting needle and paint it brown. After two or three coats, for a dark rich colour, finish off with a clear varnish to give the 'puddings' a lovely shine.

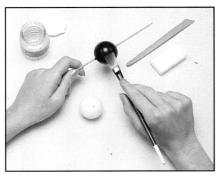

Now take some modelling clay, the sort you can bake in the oven, and roll it into a ball, the same size as the ping pong balls. Over this, mould a thick circle of white clay, to look like custard sauce. Bake this in the oven, and then remove it from the clay ball straight away, and pop it onto a pudding, so that it fits as it cools down and hardens. Don't forget to poke a hole in the top at this point.

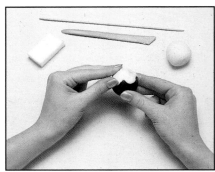

When the clay is cold, glue it to the pudding. Now take a double thread. knot the end and thread it through the pudding from the bottom upwards. Trim off the ends, then finish each pudding by gluing on foil holly leaves and red bead berries.

These little boxes make charming tree decorations. If you haven't got any suitable ones that you can wrap for the tree, you can easily make your own from cardboard. For a cube, you need to mark out a Latin cross shape. The lower arm of the cross should be twice as long as the top and side arms. Also add a 1.5cm (½ in) border to all arms except the top one for gluing the cube together.

Fold along all the lines as shown, then bring the cube together, gluing all the sides in place.

Now simply wrap the box in attractive paper, and tie it with ribbons and bows to look like a parcel. Pop it on or under the tree.

These pretty ornaments can be made any size. For a cube shape the pattern is a Latin cross (as shown), the long piece being twice the length of the others; all the other sides must be of equal length. Cut this shape out in satin, then cut a piece of iron-on interfacing, 1cm (½in) smaller all round. Iron on the interfacing. Also iron in creases to form the sides of the cube.

Placing right sides together, sew all the seams, using a small running stitch, cutting into the corners and using the interfacing edge as a seamline.

Leave one edge open so that you can turn the cube right side out. Stuff it with polyester filling, then slipstitch the opening edges together. Decorate the cube with ribbon and bows, then set it on a branch of your Christmas tree. For a rectangular box, simply widen the long section of the cross. The round box is a purchased box with satin glued onto it.

CHRISTMAS TREE TREATS

These decorations are made from a basic recipe of 250g (8oz, 2 cups) plain (all-purpose) flour, 125g (4oz, 2 tablespoons) butter, 150g (5oz, ⅝ cup) caster (fine granulated) sugar and 2 egg yolks. Cream butter and sugar until fluffy, add egg yolks and flour, and mix them into a firm dough. Roll the pasty out until it is about 1cm (½ in) thick, and cut out the chosen shapes.

Skewer a hole in each, so that you can push a thread through later. (This may close up during baking — in which case you will have to pierce another hole in them when they are cold — but very carefully, as the biscuits have a habit of breaking!) Put them onto a greased baking sheet, and bake them at 180°C (350°F), or gas mark 4, for 15 minutes.

When the cookies are cool, make up some fairly stiff icing using icing (confectioner's) sugar and water, and ice them. Thread them onto some waxed thread — or ribbon if the hole is big enough — and hang them on the tree straight away; they won't stay there very long!

Make a pattern for a Christmas stocking and cut it out double in one piece by placing the pattern on the fold of a double layer of felt. Cut a strip of fake fur to fit the stocking, about 5cm (2in) deep. Catch the fur to the felt, top and bottom, by hand, with small stitches.

Now overcast the two sides of the stocking together, starting at the ankle and working around the foot and up the front. Turn the stocking right side out.

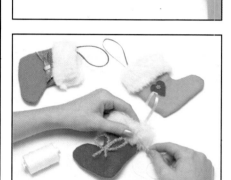

Turn the fur down about 2.5cm (1in) to the right side, catching it down around the edge. Decorate the stocking with sequins, bows, etc., and sew a loop of ribbon just inside the edge to hang it from the tree.

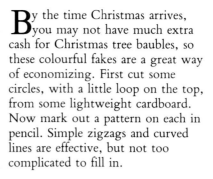

By the time Christmas arrives, you may not have much extra cash for Christmas tree baubles, so these colourful fakes are a great way of economizing. First cut some circles, with a little loop on the top, from some lightweight cardboard. Now mark out a pattern on each in pencil. Simple zigzags and curved lines are effective, but not too complicated to fill in.

Paint each bauble with several different colours, waiting for each to dry before painting the next. If you have some gold or silver paint, make good use of this, as it is very effective. Use black to make definite lines between colours.

These miniature crackers can be hung on the Christmas tree or on the wall. First take a piece of cartridge (drawing) paper or light cardboard about 8cm (3in) wide and long enough to roll into a tube. Hold it together with a little sticky tape.

When the baubles are dry, attach some thread, ribbon or, as shown, some tinsel wire, so that you can hang them up.

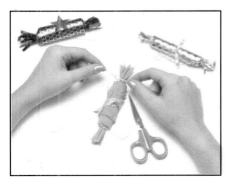

Cut a piece of crepe paper or foil twice as long as the tube, and roll the tube in it. Stick the edges together with double-sided tape. Squeeze the paper together at both ends, and tie some thread around them. Fluff out the ends and make small cuts in them to make a fringe.

To decorate the cracker, cut some extra, narrow pieces of crepe paper or foil, fringe them at the edges and wrap them around the tube as before. Alternatively, tie a bow round the cracker or stick a silver star in the middle. Tie a length of ribbon or sparkly twine to the ends by which to hang the cracker.

RING·A·DING

HANGING LANTERNS

If you haven't any shiny bells for the Christmas tree, it's not difficult to make some from foil, beads and a little string. First take a saucer and mark around it onto the back of some coloured foil. Cut out the circle, then fold it in half, and cut along the fold line. Fold each half of the circle into a cone and glue it in place.

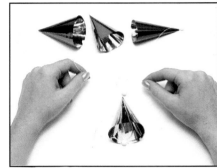

For the clapper, string a bead onto a length of thread — preferably waxed — and tie a knot over the bead. Lay the thread against the bell so that the clapper is at the right level, then tie a knot level with the hole in the top. This prevents the string from being pulled through the hole when threaded. Pull the string through the hole from the inside and thread on a smaller bead at the top; knot in place.

Finish each bell by dabbing a little glue around the bottom edge and sprinkling on some glitter. When you have made three bells, string them together, and attach them to a ring so that they can be hung on the tree. Wind a little tinsel wire around the string, and tie a couple of bows for that final touch of glamour.

These miniature lanterns make attractive Christmas tree ornaments. First take a piece of foil-covered paper 11cm (5½in) square. Fold it in half, and rule a line 1.5cm (¾in) from the loose edges. Now rule lines 1cm (½in) apart, from the fold up to this first line. Cut along these lines and open out the sheet of paper.

Hold the paper with the cuts running vertically, and glue the two sides together. When this is firm, set the lantern on the table and gently push the top down to make the sides poke outwards.

Finally, cut a strip of matching paper 13cm (5in) long and 1cm (½in) wide. Dab some glue on each end, and glue the strip onto the inside of the lantern, at the top, for a handle.

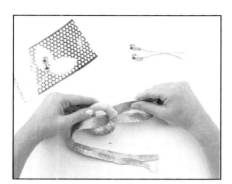

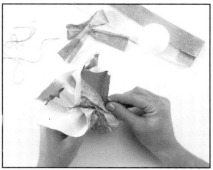

Add a touch of regal splendour to your tree with these golden decorations. To make a miniature wreath, first wind the wires of two silk leaves and two small glass balls together, and bind with white florist's tape. Cut a 16cm (6½in) length from sequin waste. Next cut a long strip of gold crepe paper, fold the edges in and bind around a small wooden ring.

Tie a loop of gold thread around the ring at the paper join. Twist the leaf and ball stems around the ring over the thread, folding in the wire ends to secure.

Fold the ends of the sequin waste into the centre so that they overlap, with the selvedges at each side. Thread a long length of fine florist's wire down the middle, through all the layers. Then thread the wire back and pull up gently to make a bow shape. Twist the wires tightly to secure and bind them around the leaf wires. Arrange the leaves, bow and balls attractively over the ring.

To make a jewelled sphere, first wrap a polystyrene ball with gold crepe paper: cut a square of paper to fit generously, and pull it up tightly over the ball. Tie firmly around the gathered paper with a length of gold thread, and knot the ends of the thread to make a hanging loop. Cut a strip of crepe paper to make a bow and fold the raw edges in. Pinch the strip into a bow shape.

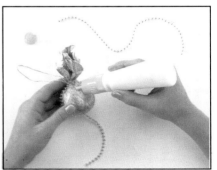

Run a line of clear adhesive around the ball and press a strip of beading trim into it. Repeat with a line of beading crossing in the opposite direction. Stick 'jewels' between the beads and large sequins, held in place with a pearl-headed pin. Trim the paper at the top of the sphere and attach the bow with a sequin trimmed pearl-headed pin.

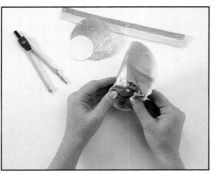

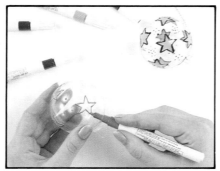

Make these delightful decorative baskets. Measure 4cm (1½in) up from the base of a yoghourt carton and cut round. Cut a 20cm (8in) diameter circle from crepe paper and cover the pot, stretching the paper up over the edges. Cover a cardboard circle with crepe paper to fit inside the base. Cut a handle 22cm (8½in) by 1.5cm (½in) from thin cardboard and wrap with crepe paper.

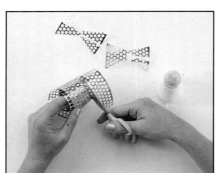

From sequin foil waste cut a strip long enough to wrap around the pot. Run a line of glue along the top and bottom of the pot and in one vertical line. Wrap the foil round, pressing into the glue, and trim, straightening the overlap along the vertical line of glue. Cut two strips 5cm (2in) wide from sequin waste, fold in half, selvedges level, and cut into bow shapes.

Staple the handle and foil bows each side of the basket. Tie bows from lengths of satin ribbon and stick over the foil bows with double-sided tape. Stick a pad in the bottom of the basket and arrange a bunch of glass baubles on top.

Here's an attractive way to add sparkle to the Christmas tree. You can buy these plain glass balls from craft suppliers, so look in craft magazines for stockists or try your nearest craft shop. As you are decorating a curved surface, it is advisable to keep the design simple. Draw the outlines of your design using a fine multi-purpose felt tip paint pen.

Try to place the motifs evenly, remembering you will see the far side of the design through the glass ball. Fill in the design with the same colour you used for the outlines. You can rub out any mistakes with a cloth soaked in turpentine.

Outline your motifs in a contrasting colour, combining colours such as red and green, yellow and black, pink and purple. Add tiny dots between the motifs using the same colour as that used for the outline. Hang the baubles from your tree with gold gift wrapping thread.

BLUE ANGEL

CHRISTMAS STAR

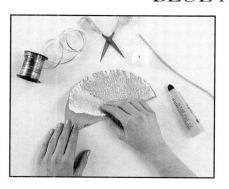

Cut a 10cm (4in) diameter semi-circle of silver cardboard, silver crepe paper and crinkly film. Trim the curve of the film in zig-zags and flute the crepe paper curve between your thumb and finger. Place the crepe paper on the cardboard with the film on top and glue together along the straight edges. Overlap the straight edges in a cone and glue.

Draw eyes with a black pen on a 3.5cm (1½in) diameter cotton pulp ball. Cut short pieces of narrow giftwrap ribbon and glue to the head as a fringe. Cut longer pieces and pull the ends over a knife blade to curl them, then glue over the head. Glue ribbon around the head, then cut a slit in the base of the head and push the cone point through.

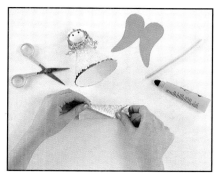

Cut silver crepe paper 11cm x 6cm (4½in x 2¼in) and flute the ends. Glue the long edges together and insert a 15cm (6in) pipecleaner for the arms through the tube and bend back the ends. Squeeze the centre and glue behind the cone, bending the arms forward. Use the template on page 163 to cut silver cardboard wings and glue them in place behind the angel.

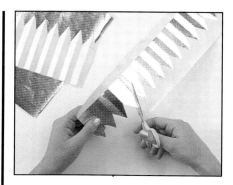

From cartridge paper cut two rectangles, one 58cm by 10cm (23in x 4in), the other 58cm by 6.5cm (23in x 2½in). Mark each one into 12mm (½in) strips and draw a line 2.5cm (1in) from the long edge. Following your marks, cut out a zig-zag edge and pleat the strips. Use spray adhesive to stick gold foil to each side of the large rectangle, and silver foil to the smaller one.

Pleat the gold strip again and fold it into a circle. Join the two ends with double-sided tape and prevent the centre from popping up by smearing glue into the centre. Weight down the star with a book until it is dry. Next make a loop from gold thread from which to hang the star, and glue this to the centre of the star at the back.

Make up the silver star as before and place a double-sided adhesive pad on the centre back. Use this to attach the star to the gold star, aligning the pleats. Finally, put a little glue into the centre of the star and press a small glass ball in place.

Cover cotton craft ball with a double layer of nylon tights. The hole in ball should be at the neck. Cut a square of nylon and stretch over ball gathering at neck, sew through tights and bind with thread to form a neck. Trim nylon if necessary. Push neck into body gathers and sew through body and neck to secure head. Sew braid around body.

For the girl: Cut 20cm (8in) narrow lace. **For the clown:** Use the green ruff. Sew short edges together and gather one long edge. Place circle over head with join at the back, pull up tightly around neck and secure thread. Tie narrow ribbon around clown's neck with bow at front.

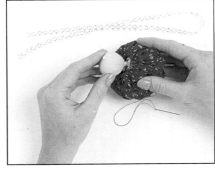

Press ½cm (¼in) to wrong side on all edges of sleeves. With wrong sides facing fold sleeve along centre length and slip stitch long edges together. Fold over 1.5cm (⅝in) at ends of pipe cleaner to make hands. Slip arms into sleeve, gather and sew fabric around wrists. Sew braid at wrists. Place arms around body with back under ruff and sew leaving front arms free.

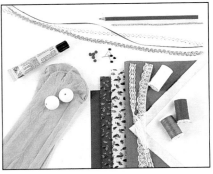

MATERIALS: *Printed cotton fabric; lining fabric; white or green fabric; decorative braids, narrow lace, narrow red ribbon; 1 × 25mm (1in) diameter cotton craft ball, 2 black map pins 1 flesh colour pipe cleaner for each doll; flesh colour nylon tights; matching sewing threads; tiny red pom poms or beads; 5cm (2in) diameter circle thin card; filling; red crayon; clear drying craft glue; pinking shears*

Sew lace around edge of right side of girl's hat. Sew running stitches 1.5cm (⅝in) from fabric edge to gather. Pull up stitches until hat fits head, add filling to crown and sew hat to head around gathers. Sew ribbon above gathers and tie with bow in front. Sew or glue pom pom or bead to centre of neck lace.

For either doll: Cut body circle 18cm (7in) diameter and sleeves 13cm x 5cm (5in x 2in) in print fabric; inner body circle 18cm (7in) diameter in lining fabric; body base circle 5cm (2in) diameter in card. **For the girl:** Cut hat circle 8cm (3in) diameter in white fabric. **For the clown:** Cut hat from print fabric; ruff 13cm x 2cm (5in x ¾in) in green using pinking shears.

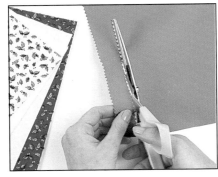

For either doll: Sew long running stitches around edge of inner body circle. Mould filling to make a ball of about 7.5cm (3in) diameter and place in centre of inner body. Pull up stitches to gather edge tightly and secure. Glue card base to cover stitches. Gather edge of body circle. Place card base to centre of wrong side of body. Pull up stitches.

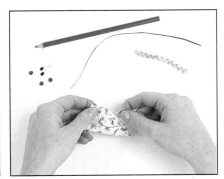

Sew clown's hat seam A–B. Turn to right side. Fill with stuffing and sew to head around edge. Sew braid to cover edge, sew or glue one pom pom or bead to front and three to body centre front. Glue back of map pins and press into head. Mark mouth in red crayon. Cut 20cm (8in) narrow ribbon, fold in centre, sew ends to body and loop to back of head to balance doll.

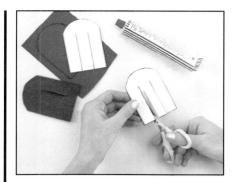

I nterweave red and green felt shapes to form hearts, adding glittery beads and sequins. Cut two templates (see page 162), from thin cardboard. Stick green felt onto one side of a template and trim to the card edges. Cut along the marked slits. Cover the opposite side of the template with green felt in the same way. Repeat the procedure, covering the second template with red felt.

Interlock the two shapes together by weaving the strips over and under their opposite number to form a heart shape.

U se shiny strands of raffia and plastic canvas circles (available from craft shops) to create these unusual tree ornaments. Weave raffia over the inner half of a 7.5cm (3in) circle with straight stitches, working each quarter section from the same central hole. The stitches will look the same from either side.

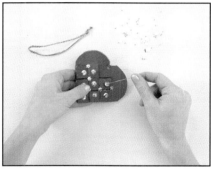

Punch a hole centrally in the top of the heart; thread with a 20cm (8in) length of gold cord and tie into a loop. Finally, decorate each side of the heart with sequins and beads; either glue or handsew them in place.

Work the outer half of the circle in the same way using the second colour. Blanket stitch around the outer edge of the circle using the same colour as the centre, tying the ends to form a loop.

On each side, handsew pearl bead trim between the two halves of the straight stitches and around the outer edge. Sew a pearl button to the centre on each side. To finish, tie a silver ribbon bow around the base of the loop.

Ring out the bells this Christmas from the tree tops. Using the pattern on page 162, cut out three side panel pieces from each of two festive fabrics. Pin and stitch the panels together, with right sides facing, to form a ring, alternating the fabrics. Cut an 8cm (3⅛in) diameter circle for the base and, with right sides facing, sew in place.

Turn the bell the right side out through the open end and fill with shredded wadding. Turn in the top raw edges and work a gathering stitch around the top; pull up tight to close and fasten off. Cut a 4.5cm (1¾in) diameter red felt circle for the clapper. Sew running stitch around the outer edge; fill with wadding and gather into a ball; fasten off. Stitch the clapper to the centre of the base.

To decorate the bell, stitch bead trim over the seamlines, beginning and ending at the edge of the base. Finally, tie a 50cm (20in) length of ribbon into a loop and tie the ends into a bow; sew onto the top of the bell.

Eight-pointed stars are a traditional Christmas design. For each side of a star, cut eight diamonds from iron-on interfacing (see page 162 for pattern). Cut two diamonds from each of four fabrics, adding a seam allowance. Fuse interfacings to the fabric diamonds and tack (baste) the raw edges over the interfacing. Oversew the diamonds together to form a star.

Make up two sides in this way and place with wrong sides facing; slip-stitch the outer edges together. Sew four lengths of braid across the seamlines, finishing one off to form a hanging loop. Finally, sew a pearl button to each point and to each indent.

A shiny foil star makes a striking decoration for the top of the Christmas tree. Using the instructions on page 35, cut out a pattern in cardboard. Now cut two squares of cardboard, slightly larger than the star template, and cover each side with a different coloured foil. Next cut out two stars, one from each foil-covered square.

This traditional English Christmas tree-top decoration makes a charming addition to the festivities. Using a saucer, cut a circle out of silver foil paper. Cut the circle in half and fold one half into a cone, taping it in place.

Take a ruler and pencil, and placing the ruler between two opposite points, mark a line on each star from one point to the centre. Cut along these lines and then simply slot the two stars together.

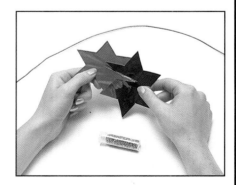

Take a pink pipe cleaner and tape it to the back of the cone; then bend it into arms and hands. On top of this fix a triangle of doily to represent wings, using double-sided tape. For the head, take an ordinary ping pong ball and skewer it onto a wooden toothpick (or cocktail stick). Push the stick into the cone.

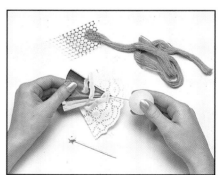

Use sticky tape to hold the points together and attach a piece of green garden wire to one set of points. You can then use the wire to attach the star to the tree. Finish the star by dabbing some glue onto the points and sprinkling glitter over them for an extra-sparkly effect.

The hair is made from grey crewel or Persian wool, stuck on with double-sided tape, and the crown is a small piece of silver sequin waste. Draw the facial features with a fine-tipped silver pen. For the wand, spray a toothpick with silver paint and stick a small silver star on one end.

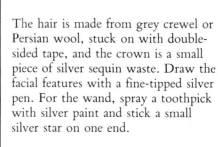

Cut a 3cm (1¼in) square of cardboard to use as a template for the doors. Draw around the square twenty-three times on the back of the tree, positioning the doors at random but leaving the trunk clear. Cut three sides of the doors, leave the right hand side 'hinged' so the door opens the right way on the other side.

On the right side of the tree, score the hinged side of each door lightly so it will open easily – but do not open the doors yet. Number the doors one to twenty-three with a silver pen.

Cut out small Christmas pictures from wrapping paper and used greeting cards. On the back of the tree, stick each picture behind a door by spreading paper glue on the tree around the doors.

Decorate the calendar with a gold star on the top and circles of metallic cardboard between the doors.

Write the number twenty-four on the front of a small red gift box with a silver pen. Stick a ribbon rosette on the top and glue the box onto the tree trunk. Fill the box with sweets. To finish, stick a picture hanger on the back of the calendar at the top.

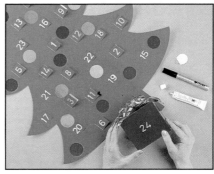

This Advent calendar can be used every year at Christmas. First make the Christmas tree pattern. Cut a piece of paper measuring about 63cm x 50cm (25in x 20in) and fold in half lengthwise. Draw half the tree with a trunk against the foldline and cut it out. Open out flat and use the pattern as a template to cut out the tree in green cardboard.

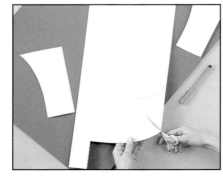

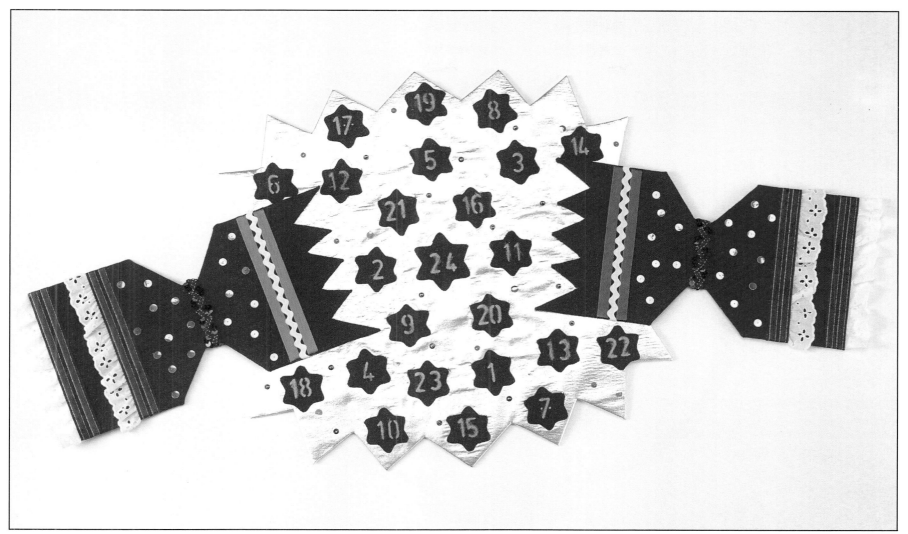

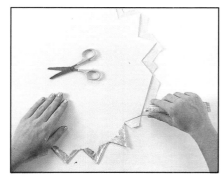

E at a chocolate a day until Christmas! Use the template on page 164 to cut out a cardboard star and iron-on interfacing. Cut out a silver fabric star, adding a 12mm (½in) allowance all around. Iron the interfacing centrally to the wrong side of the silver fabric. Cut out 24 red felt stars, making one larger, and stitch to the silver background, leaving the tops open.

Position the cardboard star centrally over the wrong side of the silver fabric. Trim the fabric allowance away at the corners and the edges over onto the cardboard, sticking in place with glue.

Cut two cardboard cracker ends, using the template on page 164. Cover with red felt, cut 12mm (½in) larger all around, gluing the raw edges over to the wrong side as before. Decorate with rows of braid, ribbons and sequins.

Position a spare piece of cardboard in each red 'pocket' in turn and stencil on a number using a silver pen and plastic stencil. Stick the cracker ends on either side of the silver star, and glue sequins between the pockets to decorate. Finally, pop a silver chocolate coin in each pocket.

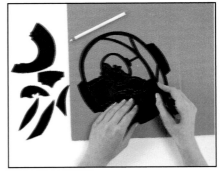

Hang this Oriental mobile at a window this Christmas and watch the winter sun shine through the coloured tissue paper. Use the template on page 162 to cut out a pair of lanterns in black cardboard. Cut out all the sections, taking care not to cut through any of the 'bridges'.

To achieve the stained glass effect, cut out coloured tissue paper a little larger than the sections to be covered. Glue the pieces of tissue paper to the back of one lantern. Trim the edges. Glue a silky red tassel to hang from the bottom of one lantern at the centre. Now glue the two lanterns together enclosing the tissue paper. Suspend the mobile on red embroidery thread.

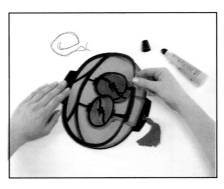

This makes an ideal Christmas wall hanging, particularly if you haven't room for a real tree. First make a paper pattern of a tree, about 75cm (30in) high and 59cm (23½in) wide at the widest point across the bottom branches. Also cut a pattern for the pot, about 25cm (10in) high. Make it about as wide as the base of the tree, with a slightly wider, 8cm (3in) deep 'rim' at the top as shown.

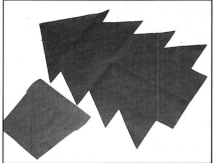

Cut out two pieces of green felt from the tree pattern and two pieces of red for the pot. Also cut out a piece of wadding (batting) for each. The wadding for the pot should be about 4.5cm (1¾in) shorter, since the rim of the pot will be turned down. On the front of the tree mark diagonal lines for the branches as shown.

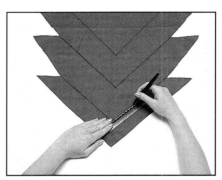

Place the tree pieces together, with wadding on top. Pin, tack (baste), then stitch 1cm (⅜in) from the edge, leaving the lower edge open. Clip the corners and turn tree right side out. Stitch along marked lines. Make up the pot, sewing up to 4cm (1½in) from the top. Turn it right side out and slip the tree inside; sew it in place. Sew the upper sides of the pot together and turn the rim down.

To decorate the tree cut out little pockets of red felt and sew them in place as shown. Insert little gifts — either real ones or gift-wrapped cardboard squares.

Finish off by adding plenty of ribbons and bells. Curtain rings also look good covered in ribbon and sewn on. Sew a loop to the top of the tree to hang it by.

Allyou really need for this decoration is some garden wire, a little bit of tinsel and a couple of baubles; but a pair of pliers will make it easier to manipulate the wire. Bend the wire into the shape of a bell. (You could, of course, try much more complicated shapes once you get the hang of it.)

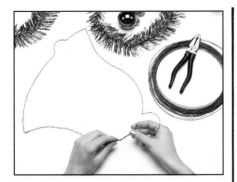

This decoration can be made with tissue paper, coloured aluminium foil, thin cardboard or construction paper. Cut between six and twelve bell shapes (depending on the thickness of the paper you use). Fold each shape in half and then open it out again.

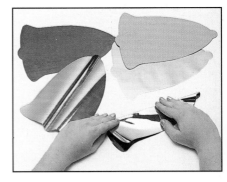

Now just wind tinsel around the wire until it is completely covered. A couple of layers will be sufficient.

Lay the cut-outs carefully on top of each other with all the creases in the centre. Now take a needle and thread, and starting at the top, make three long stitches down the middle. Bring the needle up and over the bottom to secure the shapes in place. Next make a small stitch between each long stitch. At the top, knot the two ends together.

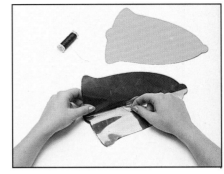

Finish off with a bauble, tied on to represent the clapper, and some bright red ribbon to tie the bells together.

Ease the bell open, piece by piece, until it forms a rounded shape. You could easily do exactly the same thing with other shapes such as a heart, ball or tree.

Heart of Christmas
Take a heart-shaped base and make an unusual but pretty display that combines a variety of natural foliage.

Garland of fir
For a decoration that can be made in moments, this simple fir and pine cone wreath looks stunning.

Cream of the crop
Use luxurious white and gold trimmings to transform a plain shop-bought wreath into a sensational showpiece.

Touch of gold
Highlight the natural beauty of greenery from your garden with golden ivy, metallic baubles and red ribbon bows.

Step-by-step to great-looking wreaths

Heart of Christmas

Finished size: About 28 x 28cm

You will need

★ Heart-shaped twig wreath or piece of strong wire bent into a heart shape
★ Selection of decorative garden foliage, including ivy, berries and flower heads
★ Roll of florist's wire
★ Red satin ribbon for hanging

1 Start by entwining lengths of ivy around the heart-shaped frame. If necessary, use short lengths of florist's wire to hold ivy in place. Build up the arrangement with a variety of foliage, threading it through and around the ivy.

2 To add interest, fix lengths of wire around the stems of flower heads and berries, then insert into the display. Thread the ribbon through the top of the frame and tie in a knot to secure. Tie the ribbon ends into a sumptuous bow and use to hang the wreath.

Garland of fir

Finished size: 55cm in diameter

You will need

★ Metal hoop or wreath frame, about 35cm in diameter
★ Roll of florist's wire
★ Fir sprigs
★ About 14 pine cones

1 Bend a 20cm length of florist's wire in half, twist the ends together and attach to the back of the frame to form a hanging loop. Trim the fir sprigs to 15-18cm long, then group into bunches of 2-3 and bind the ends together with florist's wire, leaving a long end for attaching to the frame.

2 Place a group of fir sprigs at the top of the wreath so the ends are on the left-hand side, and secure to frame with the free end of wire. Position the second group of fir sprigs below the first, so foliage covers the bound ends of the first group. Continue in this way, working in an anti-clockwise direction around the wreath, until it is completely covered.

3 Entwine a length of florist's wire around the lower scales of each pine cone and twist the ends together to form a stalk. Position the cones evenly around the wreath and secure in place with the wire stalks.

Cream of the crop

Finished size: 50cm in diameter

You will need

★ 50cm green foliage wreath
★ 6 pomanders covered in gold mesh or 6 gold-coloured pomander baubles
★ Packet of florist's stub wire
★ 15 small white pearlised baubles
★ 10 decorative pins, such as white and gold fleur-de-lys motifs
★ 2.5m of 5cm-wide wired ribbon in white and gold

1 Position pomanders evenly around wreath. Bend several stub wires in half to form 'hairpin' hooks. Attach a hook through mesh of each pomander and insert hook ends into wreath. Working from back of wreath, pull wire ends taut so the pomanders nestle within the foliage. Twist the wire ends together to secure.

2 Thread white baubles in groups of three onto hairpin hooks and position around wreath. Secure in place following same process as fixing pomanders. Insert decorative pins evenly around the wreath.

3 Cut ribbon into three equal lengths and tie each into a bow. Thread hairpin hook through the back of each bow knot and secure to wreath.

Tip: Instead of pomanders, use polystyrene craft balls sprayed gold and covered in gold mesh.

Touch of gold

Finished size: 50cm in diameter

You will need

★ 26cm wire wreath frame
★ Packet of florist's stub wire
★ Moss
★ Roll of florist's wire
★ Selection of garden foliage, including ivy and eucalyptus
★ Gold spray paint
★ 8 golden baubles
★ 10 red ribbon rosettes

1 Bend stub wire in half and attach ends to outer ring of frame to form a hanging loop. Place frame face down, then fix handfuls of moss around it with florist's wire. Turn frame face up.

2 Spray several ivy leaves with gold paint and leave to dry. Trim greenery sprigs to 12cm long, group into bunches of 3-4 and bind stems together with florist's wire.

3 Bend several stub wires in half to form 'hairpin' hooks. Starting at top of wreath and working anti-clockwise, position bunches around middle of wreath. Secure at back of wreath with a hairpin hook. If necessary, repeat with two more circles to cover entire wreath.

4 Thread each bauble on a hairpin hook; fix to wreath with ends at back. Repeat with rosettes. Wrap florist's wire around each gold ivy leaf stem and fix to display.

Fruits of the forest

Finished size: 50cm in diameter

You will need

★ 26cm wire wreath frame
★ Packet of florist's stub wire
★ Moss
★ Roll of florist's wire
★ Selection of red and orange berries, such as rosehips, skimmia and cotoneaster
★ Selection of green foliage
★ 20 lime green decorative seed pods (see Tip right)
★ Pink hyacinth
★ 10 small baubles in mauve and pink
★ Pink ribbon for hanging

1 Follow step 1 of 'Touch of gold' (right). Trim sprigs of berries and greenery to 12cm long, then group into mixed bunches of four sprigs, such as rosehips, skimmia, cotoneaster and foliage, and bind stems together with florist's wire.

2 Bend several stub wires in half to form 'hairpin' hooks. Starting at the top of the wreath and working anti-clockwise, position the bunches around the wreath, angling and overlapping them to cover the entire wreath. Secure each bunch by inserting a hairpin hook through the wreath and fixing the ends at the back.

3 Introduce contrasting colour and texture by adding chosen decorative seed pods or exotic fruits (see Tip, below). Attach a hairpin hook to each base, then position and insert evenly around the wreath, securing the hook ends at the back.

4 Carefully separate the hyacinth flower into small florets, then wire into groups and individual florets. Insert the groups around the top of the wreath and a scattering of individual florets throughout the display. Insert a hairpin hook through each bauble and, using the photo on the previous page for reference, insert around the crown of the wreath. Thread the ribbon through the hanging loop and knot to secure.

Tip: If you can't find lime green seed pods or fruits, spray paint poppy-seed heads or plain baubles. Alternatively, you could add lime green ribbon bows or artificial decorative fruit or flowers.

Photos: Thomas Dhellemmes/Marie Claire Idées, Ariadne Wonen/Samona, Knipmode/Samona, Libelle/Samona, Nouveau/Samona. Main photo styling: Veronique Villaret/Marie Claire Idées

Pull the cord and watch Santa dance. Use the template on page 163 to cut out the cardboard pieces. Cut one body and a pair of arms and legs from red cardboard. Mark the crosses on the back. Cut a pink face and glue to the head. Cut a white hat brim and beard, bobble and two cuffs. Glue the hat brim and beard over the face and the bobble to the top of the hat.

Cut out two green mittens, a black belt and two boots. Butt the straight ends of the mittens and arms together and glue cuffs over the joins. Wrap gold sticky tape around the middle of the belt and glue to the body. Glue the boot tops under the legs. Cut out a pink nose and glue on the face. Draw the eyes and mouth with felt-tipped pens.

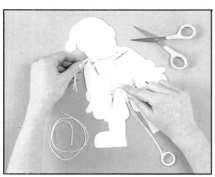

Mark dots on the limbs and attach to the body with paper fasteners at the crosses. Pull the limbs downwards on the back and tie the arms together with thread fastened through the dots. Tie the legs in the same way Thread a small ring onto a double length of fine cord. Knot the cord around the legs' thread and then the arms' thread.

Add some Christmas cheer with this festive ring. Cut a strip of crepe paper the length of the roll and bind a 20cm (8in) embroidery ring, securing the ends with double-sided tape near the hanging loop. Cut narrow gold ribbon about 110cm (43in) long and wind around the ring, securing with tape. Cut the same length from a gold sequin strip and wind between the ribbon.

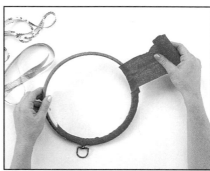

Cut crepe paper 1m (40in) long and 20cm (8in) wide; fold in half lengthways. Cut the same length from sequin waste and place over the crepe strip. Bind the centre with a long piece of florists' wire and trim ends into a V shape. Measure 23cm (9in) each side of the centre, bind with wire and fold the strip into a bow, lining up the wired points. Secure with a double-sided adhesive pad.

Use the trailing centre wires to secure the bow in position at the ring and arrange the ribbon ends over the ring. Finally, wire three small glass balls together and wrap these around the bow centre.

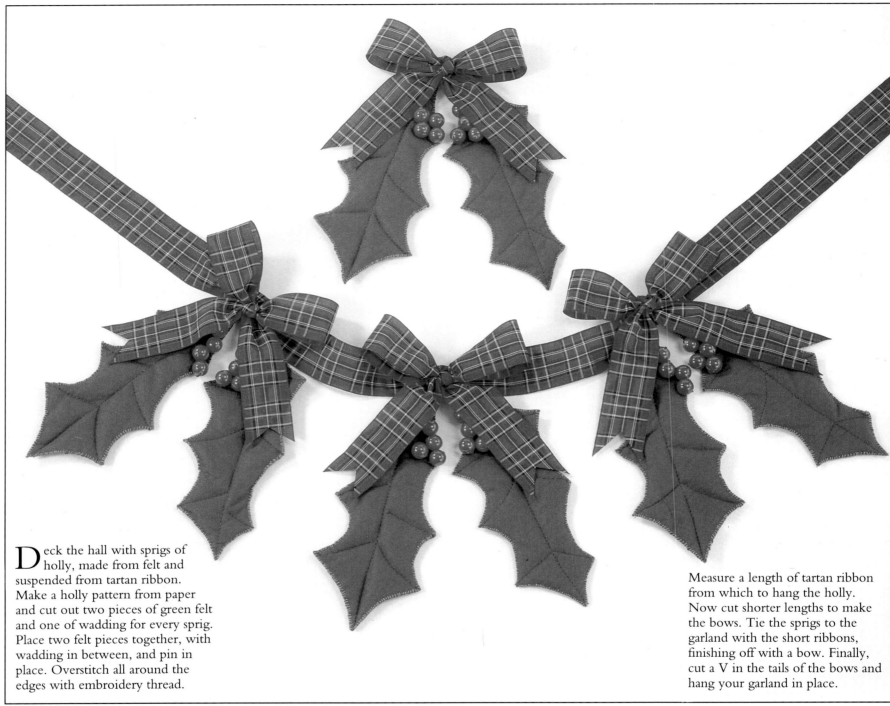

Deck the hall with sprigs of holly, made from felt and suspended from tartan ribbon. Make a holly pattern from paper and cut out two pieces of green felt and one of wadding for every sprig. Place two felt pieces together, with wadding in between, and pin in place. Overstitch all around the edges with embroidery thread.

Measure a length of tartan ribbon from which to hang the holly. Now cut shorter lengths to make the bows. Tie the sprigs to the garland with the short ribbons, finishing off with a bow. Finally, cut a V in the tails of the bows and hang your garland in place.

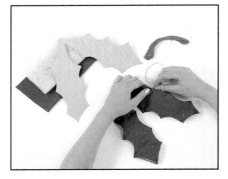

Thread your sewing machine with green cotton thread and stitch 'veins' onto each holly leaf – one down the centre and the rest sloping from the centre to the points. Next, take four red wooden or plastic beads for each leaf and sew them in place, close to the inside edge, using six strands of red embroidery thread.

This garland is made from different coloured tissue paper stars. Refer to the template on page 163 to make the basic pattern. Fold up six layers of tissue paper into quarters, place a quarter of the paper pattern on top, edges level and cut out. Fold the tissue paper in half again, (separate some of the layers if too bulky) and cut two slits in the positions marked in the photograph below. Cut a collection of different coloured tissue paper 'stars' in this way, plus two stars cut from cartridge paper for the garland ends. Glue a tissue star to each paper star using spray adhesive. Stick a small piece of double-sided tape to the centre of one tissue star and press this onto the centre of the tissue-covered paper star.

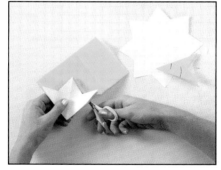

Next place double-sided tape on four opposite points of the tissue star, and stick another star on top, aligning the points and slits. Keep repeating the sequence, pressing pieces of double-sided tape alternately to the centre, then to the four points, of each star, building up the layers until the garland is the required length. Finish by attaching the other end section.

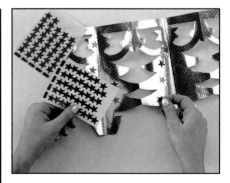

Use this attractive frieze to decorate shelves, or to hang along a wall. From a length of foil gift wrap cut a long strip 23cm (9in) wide. Make a tree template from paper using the pattern on page 163 and line it up along one short edge of the gift wrap. Draw around the outline marking a fold line down the centre of the tree shape. Mark an X on each section to be cut out.

Fold the gift wrap concertina fashion along its length and staple the layers together above and below the pattern area to prevent the folds from slipping. Cut out through all the layers, using a craft knife to cut out the enclosed areas between the star and the bell shapes. Be careful not to cut through the folds at the edge.

Open the frieze out. The foil can be left in gentle folds, or pressed flat with a cool iron. Stick self-adhesive foil stars all over the trees. You can make the frieze to the required length simply by joining several frieze strips together end to end, with sticky tape.

  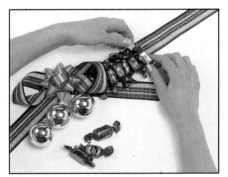 

For those with a sugary tooth, here is a garland covered in brightly wrapped sweets — to be enjoyed long after the party is over. Cut a length of ribbon about 135cm (54in) long and mark the centre. Next cut three 112cm (45in) lengths of ribbon and make them up into three bows, stapling the loops into an open position as shown and trimming the ends into points.

Tape the bows onto each end and onto the centre of the main ribbon length. Then use silver thread to hang clusters of baubles from the centre of the bows. (Hang the baubles at varying lengths for the best effect.) Glue the threads to the centre of the bows and cover them up with an adhesive ribbon rosette.

Decorate some sweets with silver stars and staple them along the top edge of the ribbon between the bows. Use double-sided tape to attach the underside of the sweets to the ribbon. Finally, sew curtain rings onto the back of the ribbon for hanging the garland.

For the rosettes, cut a circle of silver cardboard, 10cm (4in) across. Take a piece of ribbon 80cm (32in) long, fold it in half and staple it to the centre of the circle. Trim the ribbon ends into points. Staple the sweets in a circle around the cardboard as shown, then stick a ribbon star in the centre. Using sticky tape, attach a curtain ring to the back of the circle for hanging up the rosette.

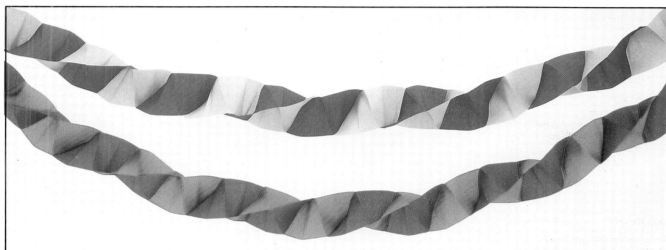

This simple paper chain takes only a few minutes to make. All you need are two different-coloured crepe papers and a touch of glue. Cut 7.5cm (3in) off the end of each crepe paper roll. Place the strips at right angles to each other, and glue one end over the other as shown.

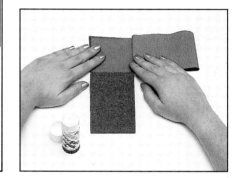

Bright-coloured foil paper makes a festive version of the simple link chain. Begin by cutting lots of strips about 18 by 3cm (7 by 1¼in). Stick the ends of the first strip together with double-sided tape (neater and quicker than glue) to make a link.

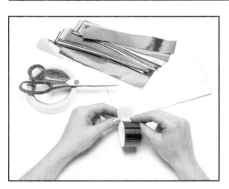

Bring the lower strip up and fold it over the other, then fold the right-hand strip over to the left as shown.

Now simply thread the next strip through and stick the ends together. Continue in this way, alternating the colours, until the chain is as long as you want it.

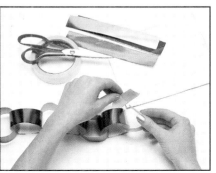

That's all there is to it; just keep folding the strips over each other alternately until you reach the end. Glue them together at the ends and trim off any extra bits.

This is another fun way to hang up your Christmas cards. Simply take three long pieces of gift wrap or woven ribbon in red, green and gold, and plait them tightly together. Knot them at each end to hold them in place.

Now take some clothes pegs, lay them on several sheets of newspaper and spray them with gold paint. Turn them until all the sides have been covered and leave them to dry.

Hanging up your Christmas cards always poses a problem. Here is a simple way to overcome it while making an interesting 'picture' for your wall at the same time. First take a piece of wooden garden trellis, extend it, and spray it with gold paint.

Fasten the ribbon to the wall at each end, and use the gold pegs to attach your Christmas cards to it. (If you prefer, and if you have some to spare, you could use tinsel instead of ribbon.)

While the trellis is drying, lay out some ordinary wooden clothes pegs and spray them gold as well. You will have to turn them over a few times so that all sides are covered.

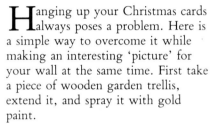

When the trellis is dry, take some thick strands of tinsel and wind them all around the edge of the trellis to make a frame. Now hang the trellis on the wall, and use the pegs to attach the Christmas cards as they arrive.

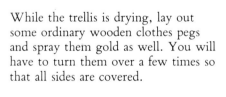

Here is a lovely sparkly garland to hang at Christmastime. Cut Christmas tree and bell shapes from foil-covered cardboard, marking the shapes out first on the wrong side. Be careful when cutting as foil cardboard tends to crinkle at the edges.

Make a tiny hole in the top of each, using a hole punch, or the tip of a skewer. Using red twine, tie each shape to a long strand of tinsel, leaving even spaces between them. At the top of each bell, fix a bow of gold-covered wire; on the trees, a little star.

The paper used for these crackers is similar in texture to curling gift wrap ribbon and has a lovely shiny satin finish. Cover empty toilet paper rolls or cardboard tubes with white sticky-backed plastic, which prevents the colour from showing through. Now cut pieces of shiny paper, twice as long as the tubes, and wide enough to go easily around them.

Wrap the tube in the paper and fix in place with double-sided tape. Don't twist the ends; scrunch them in with elastic (rubber) bands, which you can then cover with strips of curling ribbon. Decorate the crackers with boiled sweets (hard candies), stuck on with double-sided tape. Staple the crackers onto a strip of tinsel and trim the garland with sweets and baubles.

EIGHT-POINTED STAR

SNOWFLAKE

A large foil star to hang in the centre of the ceiling or over the fireplace. Try it out on a piece of ordinary paper first, as it is a little fiddly. Cut a piece of foil paper about 45cm (18in) square. Fold it in half from corner to corner, then in half twice again, making a small triangle.

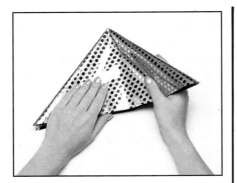

Bend the single-fold edge over to the edge with three folds. Open it out, and rule two lines from the corners at the base of the triangle to the centre crease. Cut along these two lines.

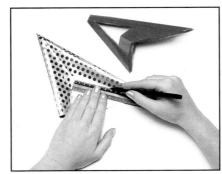

Refold the crease and rule two more lines, forming a small triangle as seen here. Cut this out. Now snip the point off and open the star out. Glue it to another piece of thicker foil paper for backing and cut the star out carefully when the glue has dried. Finish it off with a ribbon rosette in the centre.

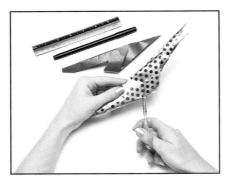

Y ou can always have snow at Christmas, even when the sun is shining outside. Make this snowflake in foil or in plain white paper and hang it over a window-pane. First take a square of paper, fold it into quarters, then in half diagonally, then lastly back on itself as shown.

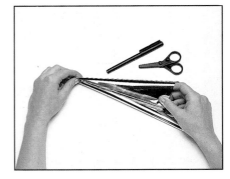

Make a pattern of the chosen design, then mark it on the folded paper with a black felt pen. Shade the areas that are to be cut away, then cut them out. Open out the snowflake. If you use a very flimsy foil, glue the snowflake onto a piece of paper, and cut out around it. This will make it easier to hang.

Finally, decorate the snowflake with sequins in bright jewel colours. The more patience you have, the more sequins you will use and the better it will look!

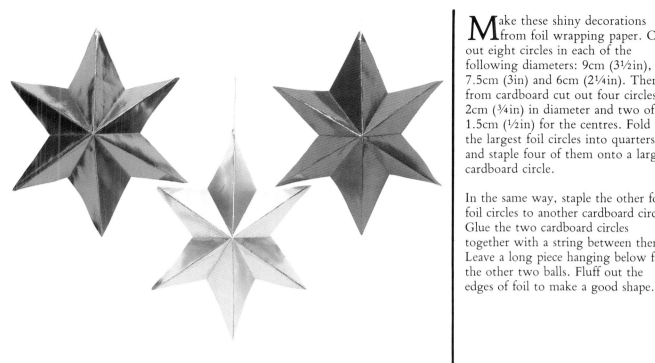

Make these shiny decorations from foil wrapping paper. Cut out eight circles in each of the following diameters: 9cm (3½in), 7.5cm (3in) and 6cm (2¼in). Then from cardboard cut out four circles 2cm (¾in) in diameter and two of 1.5cm (½in) for the centres. Fold the largest foil circles into quarters and staple four of them onto a large cardboard circle.

In the same way, staple the other four foil circles to another cardboard circle. Glue the two cardboard circles together with a string between them. Leave a long piece hanging below for the other two balls. Fluff out the edges of foil to make a good shape.

This simple star can be hung on the wall or from the ceiling. First make the pattern for the star. Using a ruler and protractor, draw an equilateral triangle (each angle is 60°). Cut out the triangle and use it as a pattern to make another one. Then glue one triangle over the other to form the star. Use this pattern to cut a star from foil paper.

Now make the other two balls in the same way, using the smaller cardboard circles for the tiniest. Fix the balls to the string as you go.

Fold the star in half three times between opposite points. Next fold it in half three times between opposite angles as shown. Every angle and point should now have a fold in it.

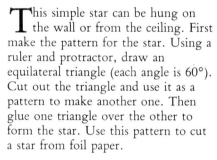

The star will now easily bend into its sculptured shape. Make a small hole in its top point with a hole punch or a skewer, then put some thread through the hole to hang it up.

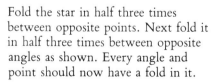

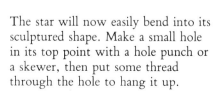

This unusual decoration adds a festive touch to a mirror or favourite painting. Make it in separate sections, one to be horizontal, the other vertical. You need fake ivy, fern and other foliage, plus pine cones, gold baubles and gold curling gift wrap ribbon. Cut off the long stems and wire everything up as shown, using florist's wire.

For the top section gradually lay pieces on top of one another, binding the wires and stems together with tape as you go along. The arrangement should be relatively long and narrow.

For the second section, use the same technique, but make the arrangement fuller. Hold the two pieces as you would like them to sit on the frame, and wire them together. Bend the stem wires back so that they will slip over the frame and hold the arrangement in place.

These small fir trees are fun to decorate and add a festive touch to any Christmas sideboard or buffet table. For a gold tree, make small bows of fine gold ribbon. Drape a string of gold beads in a spiral over the tree, starting at the top, then fix the bows in between the loops of beads.

Wrap some tartan ribbon around the pot and secure the ends with fabric glue. Make a separate bow and attach it with glue or pins.

If you have no room for a proper Christmas tree, this would be a good alternative — small but spectacular. First take a medium-sized plastic flower pot, about 15cm (6in) in diameter, and fill it, up to about 2.5cm (1in) from the rim, with fast-drying cement or wood filler. When this is just setting, insert a piece of 1.5cm (½in) dowelling about 40cm (16in) long.

When the filler is dry, spray paint the pot, the dowelling and the 'earth' surface gold. Lay it down to spray it, and when one side is dry, roll it over and spray the other side. The whole thing — especially the pot — will need a couple of coats.

When the paint is dry, take a ball of florists' foam at least 12cm (5in) in diameter and push it on top of the dowelling.

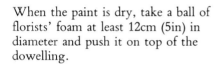

Now take short lengths of deep red and green satin ribbon, gold ribbon, shiny baubles and gold tinsel, and wire them all up, ready to push into the foam. Start with about a dozen of each; you can add to them as you go along, if necessary.

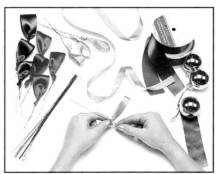

Start inserting the wires into the sphere, arranging the ribbons and baubles until it is covered, with no foam showing through. Finally wire up some curling gift wrap ribbon and insert it into the bottom of the ball. (Curl the ribbon by running the blunt edge of a pair of scissors along it.) Wind gold tinsel around the 'trunk' of the tree, and tie a large bow around the pot as a finishing touch.

Pick glittery fabrics and Christmas prints for this simple but effective wreath. Cut out lots of 8cm (3¼in) fabric squares with pinking shears. Cut a 10cm (4in) length of wire and thread a 1cm (³⁄₈in) glass bead in the centre. Pinch a square of fabric together across the diagonal and bend the wire in half across it, twisting the ends together to secure. Repeat for the other fabric squares.

Press the decorations into a dry foam polystyrene wreath, covering it completely (above). To finish, form a double bow from 3.5 cm (1½in) wide silver ribbon and secure onto the ring with wired beads (below). Cut the ribbon ends into Vs.

Dazzle your guests with an everlasting topiary tree in shades of silver and blue. Make up some plaster of Paris and fill a 12cm (5in) diameter plastic flower pot. Hold a 36cm (14in) length of 15mm (⁵⁄₈in) diameter dowel in the centre until set. Then spray the pot and the top of the plaster with silver paint.

Wind an 80cm (32in) length of silver ribbon around the dowel, fastening both ends with double-sided adhesive tape. Push a 20cm (8in) diameter florists' dry foam ball centrally on to the top of the dowel, gouging a hole in the ball first with a craft knife.

Next, make up a selection of decorations from natural materials. Stick short lengths of wire into walnuts and spray them silver. Wind lengths of wire around the base of some fir cones and spray the tips of the cones silver. Cut cinnamon sticks into 5cm (2in) lengths, wire them into bundles of three or four, then wrap the bundles with knotted silver cord to cover the wire.

Using pinking shears, cut out 10cm (4in) squares of glittery and tartan fabrics. Cut a 20cm (8in) length of wire; fold evenly in half across the diagonal of a fabric square, pinching the fabric together, then twist the ends of the wire secure. Repeat for the other fabric pieces. Stick glittery balls onto short lengths of wire.

Press the decorations into the ball until it is completely covered. We have also added artificial berries, silver acorns, wire springs and poppy seed heads. Cover an earthenware flower pot with fabric using PVA adhesive, finishing at the top with a strip of silver ribbon and a bow. Fit the plastic pot inside and a double bow of silver and tartan ribbon around the centre of the stalk.

Whether a children's party, a festive dinner party or the Christmas dinner itself, you can make the occasion a feast for the eyes as well as the palate by decorating the table with some of the stylish designs in this chapter. The centrepiece is the focal point of the table and, as such, is the most important feature. Here you will find an attractive range from which to choose, from sugared fruit and marzipan parcels to bowls of baubles and piles of mini crackers. Any of the eight beautiful napkin folds will also add style to the occasion, and most are quite easy to create. To complete each table setting, you can add some colourful name cards and present each guest with a personal gift.

Create a fully co-ordinated look for the table using traditional reds and greens. In this colourful setting, Christmas tree shapes are the prevailing theme, appearing in everything from the placemats (see page 52) to the cake. The gifts include traditional Christmas crackers (page 49) and a felt Christmas stocking containing a chocolate teddy bear (page 59) which can also double as a place marker.

Carefully roll the sheet of icing over the rolling pin and unroll it onto the cake. Shape the icing around the cake, keeping your hands wet to smooth out any cracks.

Add rows of edible cake balls to suggest garlands draped across the tree.

Place tiny red ribbon bows on the cake. (You can use a glass-headed pin to secure the bows, but take care to remove them all before serving the cake.)

Place a selection of 'presents' around the bottom of the tree — the ones used here are Christmas tree decorations.

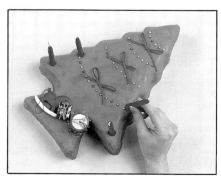

Push red wax candles into the icing around the edges of the tree to complete the effect.

This festive Christmas tree cake will be the featured attraction at a Christmas tea. The cake can be made to your own traditional recipe and should be baked in a Christmas tree cake tin. The simplest method for icing the cake is to use ready-to-roll fondant icing. Knead the block into a ball and work in some green food colouring.

Roll the coloured icing out flat on a cool surface, first sprinkling some icing, or confectioner's, sugar on the worktop to prevent the icing from sticking.

A touch of gold gives this platter of fruit and nuts extra richness. Begin by spraying ivy, clementines, bay leaves and fir cones with gold paint. (If the fruit will be eaten, make sure that the paint you are using is non-toxic.)

This centrepiece is very effective, but simple and long-lasting. If you or any of your friends have any plastic fruit that has been sitting around for some time and is ready to be thrown away, this is the perfect opportunity to give it a new lease of life. First take a deep plastic plate and spray it gold. Next take a paper doily and spray it gold also. When they are both dry, glue the doily to the plate.

Meanwhile, take a selection of plastic oranges, apples, bananas, grapes, etc., plus some fake ivy and some pine cones, and spray them either gold or bronze. Using both colours makes for variety. Let a little of their real colour come through; it adds interest. Wind the ivy around the edge of the plate, gluing it here and there to keep it in place.

Place the ivy leaves around the edge of a plain oval platter. The flatter the plate, the better, for this will allow the ivy leaves to hang over the edge.

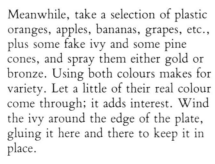

Now fill the middle with the fruit and pine cones. Again, you will have to dab a little glue here and there so that it withstands any movement.

Arrange the clementines on the platter, surround them with dates and nuts, and place a bunch of shiny black grapes on top. Add the gold leaves and fir cones for a luxurious finishing touch.

This stunning centrepiece looks grand enough to grace the most formal dinner party this Christmas, and yet is very simple to make. Using a pastry brush, coat each piece of fruit with egg white.

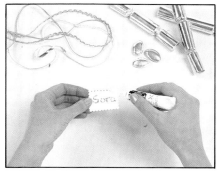

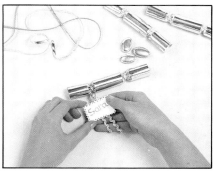

Working over a large plate, sprinkle granulated sugar over the fruit so that it adheres to the coating of egg. Alternatively, the fruit can be dipped into a bowl of sugar, although this tends to make the sugar lumpy.

These attractive miniature crackers form an eye catching centrepiece, and the surrounding sweets make a delicious accompaniment to coffee at the end of the meal. For the name tags, cut small squares and rectangles from white cardboard. Trim the edges decoratively, then write the names and embellish the edges of the card with silver or gold paint.

Cut lengths of gold and silver ribbon or braid about 15cm (6in) long. Tie a ribbon around one end of each cracker. Dab a spot of glue on the back of each name tag and press it onto the ribbon.

Ivy leaves are used here to form a decorative border; but remember to use a doily to separate the poisonous leaves from the fruit if you intend to eat the fruit later.

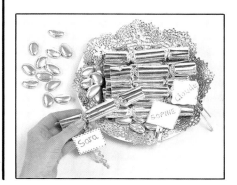

Pile the crackers onto a large plate covered with a gold doily. Place those with name cards near the top of the pile. For a finishing touch, surround the pile of crackers with gold and silver dragées.

Clementines are a favourite at Christmas, and here an attractive effect has been created by hand-painting a plain wicker basket to match the colour of the fruit. Paint the basket inside and out with a water-based paint in the background colour, using a small decorating brush. Leave the basket to dry.

Exquisite marzipan fruits deserve special presentation. Nestling in little tissue 'parcels' and piled into a cake stand, they make a colourful centrepiece. All you need is several different colours of tissue paper and some pinking shears. Instead of marzipan fruits, you could use chocolates or marrons glacés.

Dip a sponge into a saucer containing the contrasting colour of paint. Dab the sponge a few times on a piece of scrap paper to remove any excess. Then sponge all over the outside of the basket, replenishing your paint supply when necessary.

From a double layer of one colour of tissue, cut a 10cm (4in) square. Pinking shears give an attractive serrated edge. From another colour of tissue, also double, cut a smaller square, measuring about 6cm (2½in).

Arrange the fruit in the basket as shown, adding a few leaves for contrast. Clementines are shown here, but apples, bananas and other fruit could be added for variety.

Lay the smaller square on top of the larger one. Place the marzipan fruit in the centre and gather the tissue around it. Hold it in place for a few seconds and then let go; the crumpled tissue will retain its rosette shape. Place several of the parcels on a doily-lined glass or china cake stand.

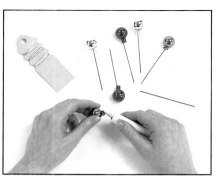

For a bright party centrepiece — ideal for Christmas or New Year's Eve — fill a glass bowl with a mixture of shiny glass baubles, foil crackers, feathers and streamers. To make clusters of small baubles, first remove the hanging string. Put a dab of glue inside the neck of each bauble and push in a short length of florist's wire. Leave them to dry.

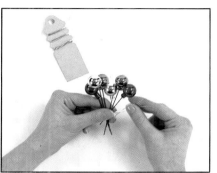

Hold the wired baubles in a cluster and wind fine fuse wire around the stems to hold them together.

Wrap a piece of shiny giftwrap ribbon around the stems and tie it into a bow. Arrange the baubles and other ornaments in the bowl as shown.

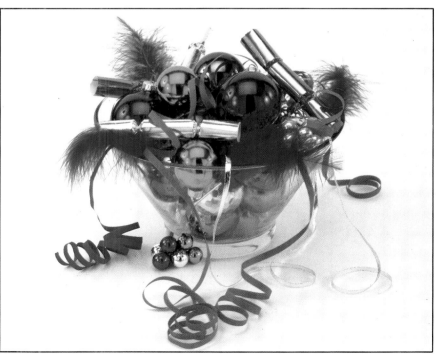

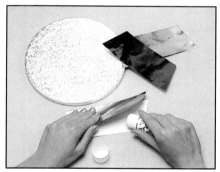

Believe it or not, this arrangement is quite simple once you get the hang of folding the cones. You need two colours of foil paper. Cut out lots of boat shapes 16.5cm (6½in) along the top and 12.5 (5in) along the bottom and about 6cm (2½in) deep. Glue one colour to another, back-to-back.

Form each boat into a cone and glue it in place. The first few you make may not look too professional, but it doesn't matter; these can go on the outside of the stand and will be partially covered. You will soon get the hang of folding the cones. Bend the bottoms under; it helps to hold the shape and looks tidier.

When you have several cones made, start gluing them around the edge of a 20cm- (8in-) diameter silver cake board. Place another two layers inside the first, leaving room for a chunky candle in the middle.

G old and silver look stunning by candlelight and this festive arrangement will flatter any table setting. To begin, spray a vine garland with gold paint, sprinkle with gold glitter, and leave to dry.

Take three flat-based candle holders and stick florists' fixative putty under each one. Position them evenly around the garland, using florists' wire to secure each holder firmly in place.

To make the silver roses cut strips of silver crepe paper 53cm (21in) by 9cm (3½in). Fold in half lengthways and tuck the short ends in. Run double-sided tape along the lower edge of a folded strip and place a wired group of gold balls at one end. Roll the crepe paper around the balls, pinching the paper tightly together at the base. Finally, crimp the petal edges to curve outwards.

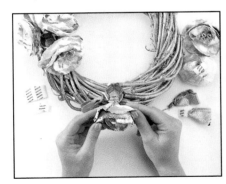

Stick a double-sided adhesive pad to the base of each rose and position four flowers around each candle holder. Cut 23cm (9in) lengths of gold ribbon and fold into double loops. Secure the ends with florists' wire and stick between the roses using adhesive pads. Tease the rose petals and gold loops to shape to hide the holders and put candles in place.

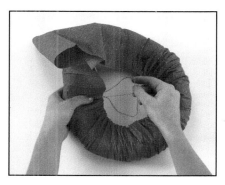

Adorn the New Year dinner table with this attractive centrepiece. Cut a length of crepe paper 120cm x 20cm (48in x 8in). Stick the ends together on the wrong side with clear sticky tape. Place a 25cm (10in) diameter polystyrene ring in the middle and sew the long edges of crepe paper together with a running stitch enclosing the polystyrene ring. Gather up the seam and fasten off.

Spray five candle holders white and push into the ring evenly spaced apart. Then drape strings of white pearls and narrow green coiled giftwrapping ribbon around the ring, gluing the ends to the underside.

Stick two rectangles of metallic blue cardboard back to back with spray adhesive and cut out five masks using the template on page 47. Score gently along the fold line of the tabs with a craft knife and bend the tabs backwards. Stick each mask by the tabs, in front of a candle.

Glue tiny blue and green star-shaped sequins to the ring, then cut out ten small stars from silver cardboard and glue between the candles and to each mask. Finally, place silver candles in the holders.

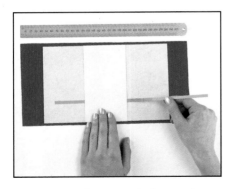

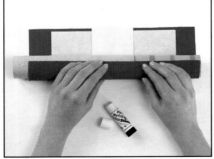

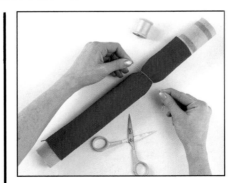

It is easy and economical to make crackers. Cut crepe paper 32cm x 16cm (12³⁄₄in x 6¹⁄₄in), keeping the grain of the paper parallel with the long sides. Lay a piece of thin writing paper 24cm x 15cm (9¹⁄₂in x 6in) centrally on top. Next cut thin cardboard 15cm x 8cm (6in x 3in) and lay it across the centre. Slip a cracker snap underneath.

Take two cardboard tubes, the sort found inside rolls of kitchen towel, and cut one in half. Lay the long tube on the lower edge of the crepe paper, with the end level with the cardboard edge. Butt a short tube against the long one and roll up tightly. Glue the overlapped edges of paper together with a low-tack adhesive.

Pull the short tube out for 5cm (2in) and tie thread tightly around the cracker between the tubes. Push the tubes together again then remove the short tube. Drop a gift, motto and paper hat inside and pull out the long tube a further 12.5cm (5in) . Tie thread tightly between the tube and cardboard inside the cracker. Untie the threads.

Cut two 25cm (10in) lengths of gold filigree lace – the kind that has a drawstring thread along one edge. Gather up the drawstring and tie the lace around the necks of the cracker. Gently stretch the ends of the cracker to flute the edges. Remove the drawstring from a length of lace and glue around the middle of the cracker. Glue a dried flower to the cracker to complete.

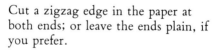

Crackers are always a must at the dinner table at Christmas. The diagram above shows the materials required for a cracker: crepe paper for the outside, tissue paper for the lining, and stiff paper and a cardboard cylinder to hold the cracker in shape.

Cut the paper layers as indicated above. Roll them around the tube, and stick them in place securely with either glue or tape. A friction strip can be placed between the stiff paper and cylinder to provide a 'bang' when the cracker is pulled.

Gather the paper together at one end and tie it with ribbon. Leave the other end open to drop in the gift, hat and joke of your choice. Tie this end and trim the ribbons neatly.

Cut a zigzag edge in the paper at both ends; or leave the ends plain, if you prefer.

Add the final decorative touches — in this case, contrasting layers of crepe paper and a paper motif.

Crepe paper

Tissue paper

Cardboard cylinder

Stiff paper

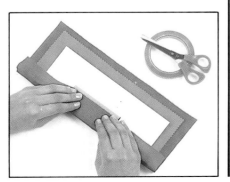

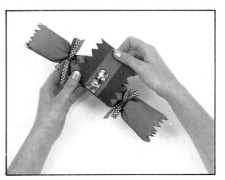

Fill this sleigh with foil wrapped candies for a charming table centrepiece. Apply gold embossed paper to both sides of thick cardboard with spray glue and cut a pair of sleighs using the template on page 163. For the base, glue gold paper to both sides of a rectangle of thin cardboard 36cm x 16cm (14⅛in x 6¼in).

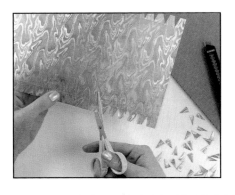

Mark the broken lines on the sleighs. Score along the base 1.5cm (⅝in) from each long edge. Snip away tiny triangles up to the scored lines so that the base will bend easily. Bend the snipped edge backwards at right angles.

Glue the snipped edges between the sleighs along the broken lines and lower, straight edges. Use the template to cut out two flowers in red foil paper and two leaves in green. Glue two leaves under each flower and glue three sequins in the middle. Glue a flower to each side of the sleigh and line it with scrunched up iridescent film.

Christmas colours are woven together to make a matching table mat and napkin set. From cartridge paper cut out a rectangle

37cm x 27cm (14¹/₂in x 10¹/₂in) and mark a 2.5cm (1in) border all round. Draw lines 12mm (¹/₂in) apart across the paper. Cut a piece of sticky-backed velour fabric a little larger all round and peel off the backing paper. Lay the the rectangle centrally on top and, using a craft knife, cut through the drawn lines as shown. Fold overlapping fabric over and stick down.

Weave lengths of green and white paper ribbon through the cut strips, arranging the ribbon so both ends pass under the border. Fold gold and silver crepe paper into narrow strips and weave over the green and white ribbon. Hold the strips in place with a little double-sided tape at both ends. Trim away the excess paper, then cover the back of the mat with sticky-backed fabric.

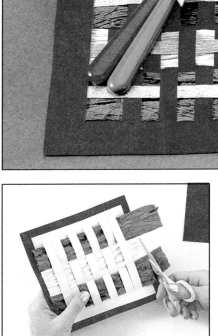

Cut a coaster mat from cartridge paper 17cm (6¹/₂in) square. Make a border as for the table mat, and mark, cover and cut in the same way. Weave with two lengths of each colour and cover the back with sticky-backed fabric as before.

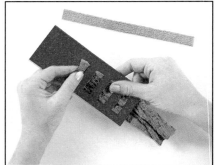

To make the napkin ring cut a strip from cartridge paper 17cm x 6.5cm (6¹/₂in x 2¹/₂in). Mark out a 12mm (¹/₂in) border and divide into strips 12mm (¹/₂in) apart. Cover with sticky-backed fabric, and cut strips as before. Weave green ribbon and silver or gold crepe through the slits and secure with double-sided tape. Cut a length of fabric for the backing and stick in place.

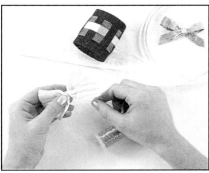

Join the two ends of the ring with double-sided tape. Make a bow shape from white paper ribbon, binding the centre with fine florists' wire. Make a small bow shape from folded gold crepe paper and stick across the white bow with double-sided tape. Stick the completed bow over the join in the napkin ring using double-sided tape.

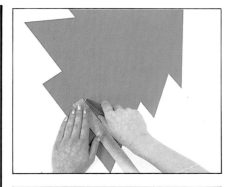

This sparkling placemat is an obvious winner for Christmas. First draw a Christmas tree on the reverse (matt) side of a piece of shiny green cardboard. The length should be about 10cm (4in) longer than the diameter of your dinner plate and the width about 20cm (8in) wider. Cut out the mat using a craft knife and a steel ruler.

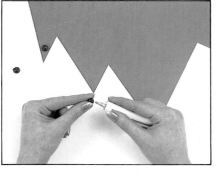

Add 'ornaments' by sticking tiny baubles to the tips of the tree using strong glue.

Add a touch of luxury to a dinner party by decorating your own tablecloth in gold. First choose a simple image, such as the fleur-de-lys motif shown here. You can either decorate an existing cloth or buy a length of wide inexpensive cotton fabric. Draw the shape in pencil first, and then go over it in gold paint.

Cut out or buy a star shape to put at the top of the tree. Finally, stick small silver stars over the mat. Or, if you prefer, just scatter the stars freely over the mat, first positioning each mat on the table.

To echo the shape of the fleur-de-lys symbol you can dress up your table napkins as shown. A napkin with a lacy edge will look best. Fold the napkin into a square. Keeping the lacy edge nearest to you, fold the left- and right-hand corners in to overlap one another. Fold the remaining point in to meet them.

Slide the napkin, lacy edge towards you, into a shining foil gift bag. Because both napkin and china are white, a lacy gold coaster was inserted into the bag, underneath the lace detail on the napkin to give it more definition.

GOLDEN TOUCH

Give a touch of luxury to plain white china by using a larger gold plate underneath each dinner plate. You will need some old white china plates, about 1.5 to 2.5cm (½ to 1in) wider all around than your dinner plates, some ivy, holly and mistletoe, gold spray paint and a few gold or silver dragées.

Place the plate on a large sheet of scrap paper and spray it with gold paint, making sure that you follow the manufacturer's instructions on the can.

Lay the holly and ivy leaves on a sheet of scrap paper and coat them with gold paint. Leave them to dry for 10 to 15 minutes, and then arrange the painted leaves on the smaller white plate with an unsprayed sprig of mistletoe for contrast. Add a few silver dragées for the finishing touch.

TASSEL NAPKIN RING

This tasselled napkin ring will add a touch of class to the dinner table this Christmas. You will need two tassels and approximately 40cm (16in) of cord per napkin, and a strong fabric glue. Attach the tassels to the cord by wrapping the loop around the cord and pulling the tassels through it.

Make the ring by feeding the cord through both loops of the tassels twice more. Make sure that the ring is large enough to slip easily over the napkin.

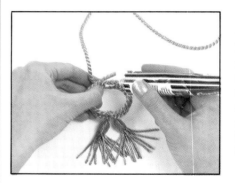

Using a strong glue, secure the ends of the cord to the back of the ring. Lay one end along the back and trim it. Having applied the glue to the inside of the ring as shown, wrap the remaining end over the cords, covering the trimmed end. Cut the remaining piece of cord on the inside, and clamp it in position until it is dry.

For best results use a crisply starched napkin to make this attractive fold. First fold the napkin lengthwise into three to form a long rectangle. Lay it horizontally with the free edge away from you, and fold the left- and right-hand ends in to meet in the centre.

Fold the napkin twice to form a square and position it with the loose corners at the top right. Fold the top corner back diagonally to meet the lower left corner, then turn it back on itself as shown. Continue to fold the corner back and forth to create a 'concertina' effect along the diagonal strip of napkin.

Fold down the top right- and left-hand corners to meet in the centre, forming a point. Take the napkin in both hands and flip it over towards you so that the point is facing you and the flat side of the napkin is uppermost.

Lift the next layer of fabric from the top right-hand corner and repeat the process described above to create two parallel strips with zigzag edges.

Lift the sides and pull them over towards one another to form a cone shape. Tuck the left-hand corner into the right-hand corner to secure it. Turn the napkin around and place it on a plate as shown in the main picture.

Pick the napkin up in both hands with the zigzag folds in the centre. Fold it in half diagonally to form a triangle, keeping the pleats on the outside. Take the right-hand and left-hand corners of the triangle and curl them back, tucking one into the other to secure them. Stand the napkin upright on a plate as shown.

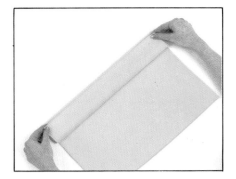

F old the napkin in half to form a crease along the centre line. Then open the napkin out again. Fold one half of the napkin lengthwise into three by bringing the top edge of the square inwards to the centre line and then folding it back on itself as shown. Repeat with the second half.

Fold the napkin in half lengthwise by tucking one half under the other along the centre line. Lay the resulting strip flat with the three folded edges facing you. Mark the centre of this strip with a finger and fold the right-hand edge in towards the centre and back on itself as shown. Repeat with the left-hand side.

A crisply starched napkin is required for this pretty fold. Lay the napkin flat. Fold two edges to meet in the centre as shown. Then fold the half nearest you across the centre line and over on the top of the other half, to form a long, thin rectangle.

Pull the top left-hand corner across towards the top right-hand corner to create a triangle, pressing down gently along the folds to hold them in place. Repeat with the remaining left-hand folds, and then do the same with all the right-hand folds. Ease the folds open slightly and display the napkin with the centre point facing the guest.

Fold the right-hand end of the rectangle in towards the centre, and with another fold double it back on itself as shown. Repeat with the left-hand side so that the double folds meet in the centre.

Pull the right-hand back corner across to the left, bringing the front edge across the centre line to form a triangle. Anchoring the right hand side of the triangle with one hand, use the other hand to fold the corner back to its original position, thus creating the 'wings' of the arrangement. Repeat the process on the left-hand side.

This elegant napkin fold is easier to produce than it looks. First fold the napkin in half diagonally, then bring the left- and right-hand corners up to meet at the apex.

This highly effective design benefits from a well-starched napkin and is very easy to make. Begin by folding the napkin in half lengthwise and then fold one end of the oblong backwards and forwards in concertina- or accordion-style folds, until just past the halfway point.

Holding the folds firmly together, fold the napkin lengthwise down the middle to bring both ends of the 'concertina' together. Keeping the folds in position in one hand, fold the loose flap of the napkin over across the diagonal.

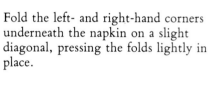

Turn the napkin over, and fold the lower corner up slightly as shown.

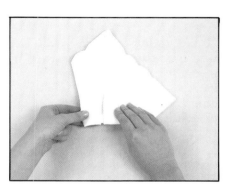

Push the flap underneath the support as shown to balance the napkin, and, letting go of the pleats, allow the fan to fall into position.

Fold the left- and right-hand corners underneath the napkin on a slight diagonal, pressing the folds lightly in place.

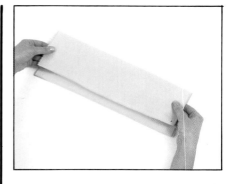

This design looks best in a conical glass but can be adapted for a wider-based container. Although it takes a little more practice than most, it is worth the effort. First lay the napkin flat and fold it in three lengthwise. Position it as shown, with the free edge on top.

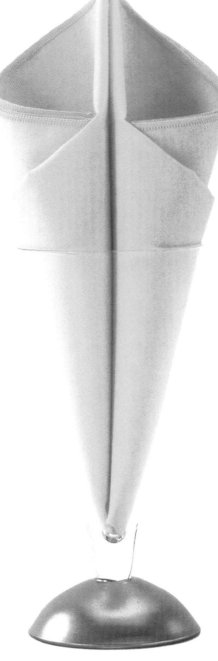

Take hold of the top left-hand and right-hand corners of the napkin with the index finger and thumb of each hand. Roll the corners diagonally towards you as shown.

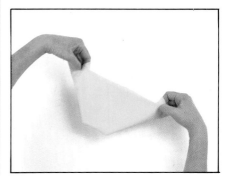

To make this graceful fold, lay the napkin flat and fold it in half diagonally to form a triangle. Position it with the folded edge towards you. Bring the top corner towards you, so that the point overlaps the folded edge slightly. Carefully turn the napkin over and repeat with the other corner.

Pleat the napkin evenly across from left to right, in accordion- or concertina-style, folds. Holding the straight edge of the 'concertina' firmly in position, arrange the napkin in a glass. Pull the front layer of the top point towards you, creating a pointed flap over the front of the glass.

Without releasing your hold on the napkin, continue to roll the corners inwards in one sweeping movement by swivelling both hands and napkin down, up and over until your hands are together palms uppermost. By now the napkin should be rolled into two adjacent flutes. Release your hands and place the napkin in a glass, arranging it neatly.

KITE PLACE CARDS

These colourful place cards are perfect for a children's Christmas party. For each kite you will need stiff paper in two colours. From each colour cut two rectangles, each 10 by 15cm (4 by 6in). Draw a line down the centre, then another line at right angles across it, 5cm (2in) from one end. Join up the points, then cut off the four corners; set them aside.

Use two of the corners of the red card to decorate the yellow kite, glueing them in place as shown. Similarly, use two of the leftover pieces of the yellow card to decorate the red kite. Write the name on each kite.

Cut out squares of coloured tissue, allowing three for each kite. On the back of each kite, glue a 40cm (16in) strip of thin ribbon. Pinch the squares of tissue together in the centre and tie the ribbon around them. Cut a small strip of cardboard, fold it in two and glue it to the back of the kite; use this hook to attach the kite to a glass.

TARTAN PLACE CARD

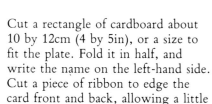

Add a truly Scottish flavour this Christmas by making these tartan place cards for your guests. Use plaid ribbon and either white or coloured lightweight cardboard, and add a kilt pin for the finishing touch.

Cut a rectangle of cardboard about 10 by 12cm (4 by 5in), or a size to fit the plate. Fold it in half, and write the name on the left-hand side. Cut a piece of ribbon to edge the card front and back, allowing a little extra to turn under the edges.

Stick ribbon onto the card with fabric glue, folding the excess underneath as shown. Pin the kilt pin through the ribbon and card to complete the authentically Scottish look.

PASTRY PLACE MARKER

TEDDY PLACE MARKER

Here's a novel way to show guests where to sit — a pastry place marker shaped like a Christmas tree. Make the dough by mixing three parts of white flour to one of salt, a spoonful of glycerine and enough cold water to give a good consistency. Knead the pastry for about 10 minutes, then roll it flat on a floured surface.

Cut out the shapes with a sharp knife or a pastry cutter. Remember to make a hole for the ribbon. Bake the pastry in the normal way.

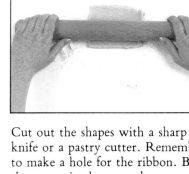

Either leave the shapes plain or colour them with water-based paint. You can pipe your guests' names on using tube paint. Varnish the shapes (optional) and attach a ribbon. Note that these pastry shapes are not edible and should be used only for decorative purposes; however, they will keep for years. They can also be used as Christmas tree ornaments.

For a children's party at Christmas this ingenious place marker is sure to be a winner. First, cut two boot shapes from bright-coloured felt, making sure that they are large enough to enclose a chocolate teddy or other favour. Stick the shapes together with fabric glue, leaving the top open.

From contrasting felt, cut a zigzag strip for the upper edge and some letters to make the name.

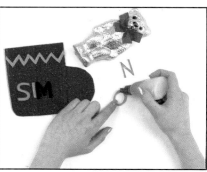

Glue the strip and the letters to the boot as shown. Finally, insert the chocolate teddy into the boot.

Miniature holly sprigs give a festive touch to a place card. From thin cardboard cut a rectangle 7.5cm x 10cm (3in x 4in). Gently score across the centre, using a craft knife against a ruler, and fold the card in half. Punch a hole in the lower left side. Make a holly leaf template from thick paper and draw around the edge on to thick green paper (artist's Canson paper is ideal). Cut out.

Score lightly down the centre of each leaf and bend to shape. Bind a bunch of red flower stamens (available from craft shops) together with fine florists' wire and cut in half across the stems to create two bunches. Bind the stamens to the front of the leaves with red florists' tape.

Fold a short length of narrow curling ribbon in half, at a slight angle, and secure fold with a small piece of double-sided tape. Curl the ribbon against a scissor blade and stick to front of the holly sprig. Write the name on the card and push the holly sprig through the punched hole, securing the stems to the back of the card with a small piece of sticky tape.

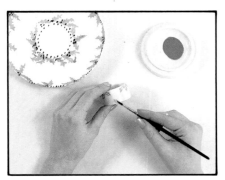

Choose a simple motif, such as holly, mistletoe, or bells, and create your own unique festive tea service. For this attractive holly design, you will need plain white china, red and green ceramic paint and a fine paint brush. Paint the outlines of the holly leaves with green paint, grouping the leaves together in threes. Now fill in the leaf outlines with more green paint.

Join up the leaves with garlands of red berries made by applying dots of red ceramic paint with a very fine brush. Also add clusters of berries at the base of the leaves. When the paint is completely dry, finish off with a coat of ceramic varnish. To complete the picture, you can even paint the motif on to the corner of your paper napkins.

For an unusual centrepiece, fill a basket with festive fabric balls. Cut a holly leaf shape from medium weight interfacing. Cut a strip of fabric twice the length of the leaf and stitch the interfacing to the wrong side. Fold the fabric over the leaf and stitch over the previous stitches. Cut out with pinking shears. Make three more leaves, add beads for berries and sew to the basket.

Make up a 3cm (1¼in) wide frill by cutting a fabric strip twice the length of the basket top by 8cm (3¼in). With wrong sides together, fold in half lengthways so raw edges overlap in the centre; sew running stitches along the length and gather. Pull up to fit the top of the basket and handsew in position, neatening the ends together. Wrap glittery cord around the basket handle.

For each ball, cut a 20cm (8in) fabric circle with pinking shears. Wrap around a 5cm (2in) compressed paper ball, pleating up the fabric evenly. Cut a 25cm (10in) length of ribbon; gather along one edge with running stitch, pull into a rosette and fasten off. Pin to the top of the ball, through all layers of fabric, with a glass-headed pin threaded through a star-shaped sequin.

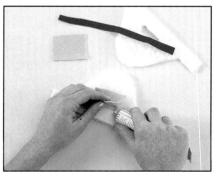

Lay a festive table with a cheery napkin ring for each guest. Cut out one pattern piece (see page 162) from white fur fabric, a piece of flesh-coloured felt 5.5cm x 4.5cm (2¼in x 1¾in), and a 15cm x 1cm (6in x ⅜in) strip of red felt. Stick the flesh-coloured felt centrally across the back of the opening on the fur fabric to form the face.

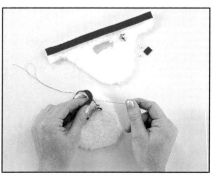

Now glue the red felt strip across the top of the fur fabric piece. Stick on two small eyes and a square of red felt for the nose. Fold the side panels back to form a ring, overlapping them by 1cm (⅜in), and glue. Finally fasten a bell to one side of the red band with a length of 'worked' thread, sewing a few strands between the band and the bell and working over them with buttonhole stitch.

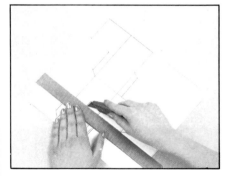

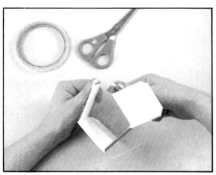

Little boxes, decorated with tissue paper pom-poms and filled with candies, make lovely gifts at the Christmas table. To make the pom-pom, fold some tissue paper to get at least 12 layers, measuring 7cm (3in) square. Using a cup or glass, mark a circle on the paper, and cut it out. Staple the layers together at the centre.

Cut strips into the centre, making them about 5mm (¼in) wide at the edge and stopping short of the staple. Fluff up the tissue paper to form a pom-pom, and glue it to the box. To make the box, copy the template below and then refer to the instructions adjacent (i.e. those for the square gift box).

This elegant little box is ideal for wrapping a special gift for each of your dinner guests this Christmas. First draw the diagram to the specified measurements, then trace it. Tape the tracing to the wrong side of medium-weight cardboard with masking tape and draw over the outline to make a light indentation in the cardboard. Cut around the outline.

Score the fold lines carefully with scissor points and fold the box accordingly. Apply glue to the flaps and join the box together as shown. Allow it to dry thoroughly before using it.

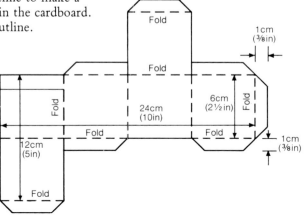

Give each of your guests a little table gift this Christmas, wrapped up in some pretty fabric. Fine scented soap makes a perfect gift for the ladies. Cut a 15cm (6in) square of fabric, using pinking shears for a decorative edge and to prevent fraying.

A stunning, yet simple, idea for a festive dinner party, these net bags contain sweets for your guests. Cut a large gold doily in half. Fold the edges around to meet one another, creating a cone shape, and then secure them with tape.

For a gift bag, place the soap in the centre of the square of fabric. Gather the corners together in the centre. Tie a contrasting ribbon around the fabric and into a bow. For an envelope, fold the four corners of the square over the soap to overlap in the centre.

Cut out a square of black dressmaker's or milliner's net. Use it double for a fuller effect. Holding the net square in one hand, place the gold doily cone into it. Place three or four black and gold dragées in the cone.

Hold the flaps of the envelope in place and tie them up with a contrasting ribbon. Finish off with a large bow.

Gather the net and doily cone into a 'waist', leaving some extra at the top. Secure it with sewing thread, wrapped tightly around it several times, or with an elastic band. Cut equal lengths of thin gold and black ribbon, and tie them around the waist and into a bow at the front.

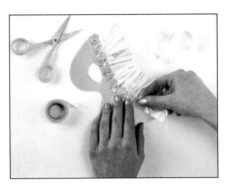

Be the belle of the ball with a lavishly jewelled mask. Spray glue two pieces of gold cardboard together for extra strength, then use the template on page 163 to cut out the mask. Stick double-sided tape to the top edge on the back of the mask. Cut a strip of iridescent film 50cm x 6cm (20in x 2¼in). Scrunch up one long edge and press onto the tape.

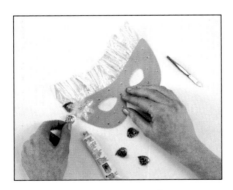

Glue an iridescent plastic flower to the left-hand corner. Glue small glass stones at random to the mask and stick one in the centre of the flower. A pair of tweezers is useful for holding tiny stones. Glue gold plastic leaves around the flower.

Spray a 30cm (12in) length of thin wood dowel gold and bind with narrow giftwrap ribbon. Glue the ends in place. Pull two lengths of giftwrap ribbon between your thumb and finger to coil them. Stick the ribbons to one end of the dowel with sticky tape and use a strong glue to stick the wooden handle behind the mask.

Here's a jaunty majorette's cap that is ideal for a fancy dress party. Cut a strip of coloured cardboard 60cm x 13cm (24in x 5in). Use the template on page 163 to cut out a peak in silver cardboard. On the wrong side, score the peak along the broken lines and make snips in the cardboard to the scored line. Bend the snipped edge upwards.

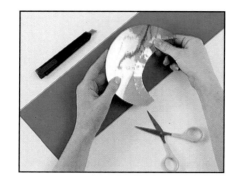

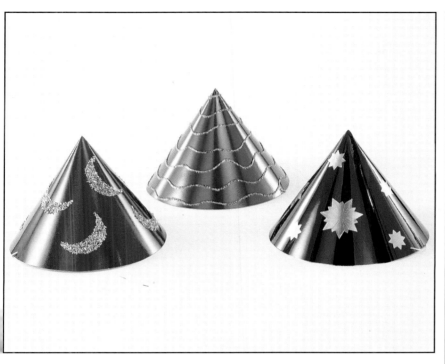

Stick an 18cm (7 in) long strip of double-sided tape in the middle of one long edge of the hat on the wrong side. Overlap the ends of the strip and lightly hold together with masking tape. Press the snipped edge of the peak onto the sticky tape. Remove the masking tape.

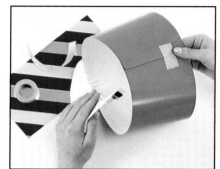

These conical hats are so easy to make that you will want to make one for each of your party guests. Cut a 30cm (12in) diameter circle of shiny cardboard for each hat and cut to the centre. Cut a slice out of the circle so that the hat is not too bulky. Overlap the cut edges and glue together.

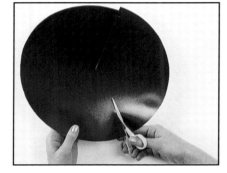

Wrap the hat around your head, overlapping the ends, and stick together with double-sided tape. Pleat a rectangle of foil giftwrap and bind the lower edge closed with clear sticky tape, forming a fan. Glue to the front of the hat. Finally, cut out a diamond shape from silver cardboard and glue it over the fan.

There are many ways to decorate the hats – stick on gold stars or use glitter pens to draw a pattern. Another idea is to spread glue in moon shapes on the hat and then sprinkle on glitter, shaking off the excess.

Make a hole with the points of a pair of scissors each side of the hat and thread with hat elastic. Adjust the elastic to fit under the chin and make a knot behind the holes.

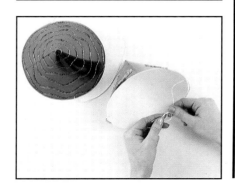

For those who prefer more natural Christmas decorations flowers are a must, providing all the colour and festive splendour anyone could want. Fresh flowers are glorious but dried flowers are so much more durable — surviving the whole festive season and on to the next! And, as this chapter shows, dried flowers are so versatile, ideal for decorating anything from wreaths and centrepieces to coasters and candlestick holders. To help you identify the plants used, a list of both common and Latin names has been provided on page 167.

Most arrangements are supported by either florists' foam or wire mesh. The foam comes in two forms — one for fresh flowers (designed to absorb water), the other for dried flowers. The latter comes in several shapes and sizes — spheres, blocks and cones — and can be cut down to any size required. Dry moss is also used as a support — packed inside a wire mesh frame to form a solid 'cushion' or bound on to a wreath frame with reel wire. Other than these supports, you will also need a sharp knife, a strong pair of scissors or secateurs and, for the dried flowers, some wire — stub wires (which come in various lengths and thicknesses), black reel wire and silver rose wire.

WIRING TECHNIQUES

Some dried flowers — yarrow and larkspur for example — have strong, firm stems that need no support. Others, such as helichrysums, have weak stems that cannot withstand the weight of the flowerheads. In the latter case, wire can be used to support the flower. Cut a stem down to about 4cm (1½in) and place it against the end of a stub wire. Then bind the length of the stem to the wire using silver reel wire.

To increase the impact of colours in a display, flowers are frequently tied into small bunches before they are arranged. To do this, cut down the stems of two or three flowers — weak stems should be cut down to about 4cm (1½in); strong ones can be left longer. Take a length of stub wire and bend back the top 3-4cm (1-1½in) to form a hair-pin shape. Place the pin against the end of the stems, bent end towards the flowerheads. Then, starting about half way down the pin, begin to wind the long end of the wire around both the stems and the short end of the wire. Bind it about three times as shown below, then straighten it so that it forms a 'stem'. Trim the wire to the required length and insert it into the display.

To give flowers more impact in a display, wire them into small bunches before arranging them. First bend the end of a stub wire to form a hair-pin shape.

Cut the flower stems short and place them against the pin. Wind the long end of wire round about three times then straighten it to make a 'stem'.

Transfuse the atmosphere this Christmas with the sweet scent of lavender and pot-pourri by making this charming basket. Begin by wiring small bunches of lavender — about three to four stems each. Attach a bunch to the rim of the basket, wrapping the wire through the wicker work. Position the next bunch over the stems of the first to cover the wires. Continue round the rim.

A collection of brilliantly coloured flowers makes a striking display for the sideboard. Begin by moulding some wire mesh into a three-dimensional shape, keeping the base flat and the top end open. Pack the mesh with dry moss, then close up the open end. Now insert wired bunches of stirlingia — tall, upright stems at the top, shorter, horizontal ones lower down.

When the rim is fully covered, cover the handle in the same way. Add a splash of colour to the display with wired bunches of small red helichrysum (everlasting or strawflower). Attach them at intervals to the rim of the basket, using the same method as before. Put two more bunches on the handle.

Next, arrange a few stems of blue larkspur around the top, and shorter bunches of blue statice lower down, following the general pattern set by the stirlingia. Follow with wired bunches of pink-dyed quaking grass, breaking out of the outline, and a few clumps of blue-dyed *Leucodendron brunia.*

Make a single bow out of deep red ribbon and wire it on to the middle of the handle. Cover the wire with a strand of lavender, fixing it in place using fine silver rose wire. To finish, fill the basket with pot-pourri, choosing a type that complements the colours of the arrangement.

Once you are happy with the general shape of the arrangement, start to fill in with bunches of large pink helichrysum (strawflower or everlasting). Pack them deep into the display. Add bright yellow highlights next with bunches of cluster-flowered helichrysum.

Finally, wire together a few bunches of rich red roses and scatter them throughout the display. It is important to position the roses last, because this ensures that the heads remain well exposed.

An attractive winter's wreath in muted creams and golds makes a pleasant change from the usual seasonal reds and greens, and gives a different and stylish Christmas decoration. Begin by covering a wreath ring in moss, packing the dry moss around the frame and binding it firmly in place with black reel wire.

Wire together some clumps of cream sea lavender and virtually cover the entire ring with it. Next, take some purple statice and wire together several bunches.

Intersperse the purple statice evenly amongst the cream coloured flowers which form the base of the garland. Then, place at regular intervals some wired clumps of yarrow and rhodanthe (sunray).

Finally, gather about 10 to 12 cones and wire them together in a large bunch. With more wire fix the cones to the wreath at the front. Pull a few strands of the flowers between the cones to add contrast. Intersperse a few more cones throughout the wreath as shown to complete the picture. This combination of flowers and cones is remarkably inexpensive, yet the result is quite stunning.

Hang this brilliant golden wreath on your front door this Yuletide to provide a colourful welcome for all your guests. It is possible to make your own base for the wreath as described opposite, but a florist should be able to provide you with a sturdy woven cane base, such as this one, for a small cost.

Wire up plenty of colourful flowers, either singly or in bunches, depending on their size. Allow plenty of wire for attaching them securely to the base. The flowers used here include helichrysum (strawflowers or everlasting), yarrow and sea lavender.

Pine cones can easily be wired around the base. Choose small closed ones for the best effect. If you cannot collect the cones yourself, your florist or a shop selling dried flowers will probably have some, and they should cost very little.

Some dried flowers come ready-wired, which makes the work easier, but a little more expensive. When everything is ready, begin wiring the various items onto the base, laying them all in the same direction.

Some flower heads will be very delicate and break off. If so, simply dab a little glue on the back and stick them on. If you start to run out of dried flowers, or you want to save some money, heather from the garden can be included; it will dry naturally once it is in place.

This unusual and imaginative wreath makes a striking decoration to hang on the door during the festive season. To create it, you will first need to buy a twig wreath from your local florist. Begin the arrangement by wiring small bunches of oak leaves together. Also take a few pieces of sponge mushroom and push wires through one side.

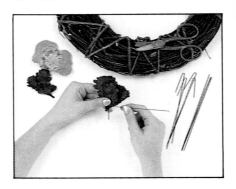

Attach the leaves and fungus to the wreath, forming three groups evenly spaced around the ring. Now wire up some lotus seedheads – wiring the large ones singly and the small ones in groups of two or three. Insert these in amongst the other plants.

Push short lengths of wire as far as they will go through one end of some walnuts. Form small groups of about three to four nuts each by twisting the wires together. Slot the walnuts into the three groups of plants. Next add a few witch hazel twigs, allowing them to break out of the arrangement and cover some bare patches between the groups.

To finish, wire together several bunches of yarrow and slot them into the arrangement, using them to close up the gaps slightly between the three main groups. The yarrow adds necessary colour to the wreath and brings it to life.

This sophisticated garland makes a stunning decoration to hang on a wall or sit on a side table. Insert four pairs of large dried flowers (we have used Carlisle thistles) evenly spaced apart in a florists' dry foam ring. Arrange white sea lavender between the flowers, virtually covering the ring.

Next, insert some cream-coloured teasels, followed by gold sprayed seed pods, artificial leaves and large wired fir cones, evenly spread throughout the garland.

Any gaps can be filled with cream helichrysum (strawflowers or everlasting) and small seed pods and fir cones. To wire the flowers, place a stub wire against the stem and bind them together close to the top with reel wire. Break off the extending end of the stem.

This stunning wreath, with its wealth of contrasting colours and materials, makes a beautiful decoration to hang on the door during the festive season. Begin by making a base using a wire wreath frame and some dry moss, binding the moss firmly on to the frame with black reel wire. Cover the base with green wreath wrap.

Take some colourful fabric and cut it up into rectangles. Now wrap about 8 to 10 small foam spheres in the fabric, gathering the material at the top and securing with wire. Leave long wire 'tails' for attaching the balls to the frame. Position the spheres in groups of two or three at regular intervals around the wreath.

Wire clumps of green amaranthus (love-lies-bleeding) and insert them into the wreath, keeping them generally quite close to the fabric spheres.

Next, wire clumps of white larkspur and intersperse these amongst the amaranthus. These reflect the white in the fabric and add highlights to the arrangement. Wire together several groups of cones and place them standing upright in the arrangement so that they do not get lost among the other plants.

Soften the display by scattering bunches of soft pink rabbit's or hare's tail grass throughout. The seeds tend to moult very easily so be careful when wiring and inserting the grass not to overhandle it.

Pick out the colours in the fabric by dotting clumps of rust coloured nipplewort (or broom bloom) throughout. The dark tones will also add depth to the display.

Finish off with a few colourful satin bows, binding each bow together with wire rather than actually tying it. Insert the bows in amongst the fabric spheres, trailing the tails prettily over the arrangement.

This striking tartan wreath makes a charming centrepiece for the table at Christmas and New Year. First you will need to buy a twig ring from a florist. Begin by individually wiring several heads of red rose. Arrange these in three small groups, evenly spaced around the ring.

Next, wire together nine small bunches of anaphalis (pearl everlasting) and push them into the ring so that they surround the roses. Take three lengths of tartan ribbon and make three single bows, wiring them together rather than actually tying them.

Take a fourth piece of ribbon, fold it in half and push a piece of wire through the folded end: this will form the long 'tails' of the arrangement. Cut a 'V' shape in the ends of the ribbons to finish them neatly, then wire a bow into each of the three gaps between the flowers. To complete the picture, wire the tartan tails beneath one of the bows.

Add several sprigs of holly, again securing them with wire. If the holly is a bit short of berries, you can add some fake berries at this point.

To hang the wreath you will need two lengths of satin ribbon. Each piece should be twice the length of the drop from the ceiling to your hanging height, plus an extra 20cm (8in) for tying around the wreath. Tie each of the four ends opposite one another around the wreath so that the two lengths cross in the centre.

Make four bows from the same colour ribbon and pin them to the wreath over the four tying-on points.

Gently push a length of florist's wire through each of four red wax candles, approximately 1.5cm (½in) above the bases, as shown.

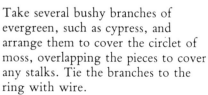

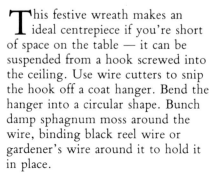

T his festive wreath makes an ideal centrepiece if you're short of space on the table — it can be suspended from a hook screwed into the ceiling. Use wire cutters to snip the hook off a coat hanger. Bend the hanger into a circular shape. Bunch damp sphagnum moss around the wire, binding black reel wire or gardener's wire around it to hold it in place.

Take several bushy branches of evergreen, such as cypress, and arrange them to cover the circlet of moss, overlapping the pieces to cover any stalks. Tie the branches to the ring with wire.

Position each candle halfway between two bows, and twist the wire around the wreath to hold it in place. To hang the wreath, tie another length of ribbon around the two main ribbons where they cross, make a loop to go over the hook, and tie the ends in a bow.

A traditional wreath on the front door gives a warm welcome to Christmastime callers. To begin, take a wire coat hanger and pull it into a circle. Bend the hook down to form a loop.

Now wire together small bunches of holly, spruce and other foliage. Then attach each bunch to the circle. Be careful when handling the holly; you can get a bit scratched, and some people can come out in a rash from it. Keep going in one direction until the whole circle is covered.

On top of this add some wired pine cones and, for extra colour, some curly red ribbon. (Use curling gift wrap ribbon for this, running the blunt edge of a pair of scissors along it to make it curl.) Red holly berries look great if you can get hold of them, but they tend to drop very quickly, so they would need replacing often. Finish off with a big red satin bow.

This sort of arrangement always looks very hard to achieve, but in fact it is very simple, provided you assemble everything you need before starting. What you need is a ring of florists' foam with a plastic base, which you can get from a florist. Also buy three plastic candle holders; stick these into the foam.

You will need holly, ivy and fern, all of them either real or fake, plus a selection of dried flowers. Used here are daisy-like sunrays, yellow helichrysum (strawflowers or everlasting), yarrow, safflowers and sea lavender. Simply break pieces off these and stick them into the foam. Try to space the flowers evenly in between the foliage.

When you have finished, stick three candles into the holders already placed. If any of the foliage is real, make sure to keep the foam damp.

IVY CANDLE-RING

FOREST FOLIAGE

This elegant candle-ring is the ideal centrepiece for a festive dinner party but it will only remain fresh for the one occasion. A circular cake base serves as the foundation for the arrangement. Begin by attaching strands of ivy to the edge of the base, securing them with drawing pins.

Build up the ring by adding more strands and bunches of leaves until only a small space remains in the centre. Push stems of freesia among the ivy leaves to provide colour contrast.

Use a mixture of white and green candles of varying heights to form the centre of the arrangement. Secure each candle to the base with a blob of glue or Plasticine (modelling clay).

The sideboard, as well as the table, needs a little dressing up at Christmas. This is bright and cheery, and the materials are quite easy to get hold of. If you don't have woodland nearby your florist should have small sections of bark for sale. Also buy a plastic candle holder. Onto the bark first put a large lump of green Plasticine (modelling clay), and on the top stick your candle holder.

Now take some plastic or silk fern and spray it gold. Break off pieces when it is dry, and stick them into the Plasticine. Also wire up strands of red paper ribbon, pine cones and red baubles and stick these in.

When the Plasticine is artistically concealed, pop a red candle in the holder, and set the arrangement on the sideboard. Put a mat under it, though, or it will scratch the surface.

A̲dd style to the dinner table with this traditional red and green centrepiece. Take a flat circular base — a cork mat or cake base will do — and glue single ruscus leaves around the edge. Stick three blocks of florists' foam on top, keeping one taller than the others. Now insert the red candles into the foam, cutting them down as necessary to vary their heights.

Build up the arrangement using gold-sprayed poppy heads, white helichrysum (strawflower or everlasting) and more ruscus leaves. The white adds essential highlights to the arrangement. Finish off by scattering single red roses throughout the display.

T̲his attractive 'woodland' design makes the perfect centrepiece for those wishing to create a more rustic effect this Christmas. Begin by making a base out of three large dried leaves, such as these cobra leaves. Glue the leaves together, then glue a block of florists' foam on top. Wire up several cones and walnuts, forcing the wire through the base of the nuts as far as it will go.

Wire together clumps of oak leaves and build up the outline of the display. Now insert the nuts and cones, placing the former in small groups. Keep the shape irregular to make it more interesting. Brighten the display by scattering small clumps of ammobium (sandflower) throughout. To finish, trim a candle to the required length and push it firmly into the foam.

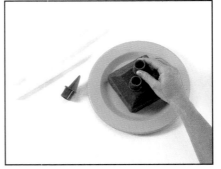

H ere is an exotic arrangement to grace the supper table. Cut a slice of florists' foam and glue to the centre of a plastic plate, then trim away the upper edges diagonally. Dampen the foam. Push three candle holders into the top, forming a ring, and insert three white candles of varying heights. Arrange short lengths of trailing ivy to hide the holders.

Push large ivy leaves into the foam to cover the plate as shown above then arrange apples on cocktail sticks around the foam. Next, place small bunches of grapes between the apples, securing them to the foam with stub wires bent in half. Fill any gaps with chincherinchee flowers and individual grapes on cocktail sticks as shown below. Be sure to wash the fruit afterwards if you intend to eat it.

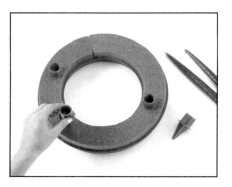

This festive table centrepiece is inexpensive to produce as the foliage used can be found in abundance during the Christmas period. Take a florists' foam ring and insert four candle holders evenly spaced around it.

Dampen the ring and insert four red candles in the holders. We have used hand-made candles for added interest. Now push sprigs of yew into the ring, positioning all the foliage in the same direction.

Next, take four large fir cones and bind wire around the base between the lower scales leaving a long length of wire to insert into the ring. Push the cone wires into the ring between the candles.

Finally, add sprigs of holly and berries to the ring. Berries can be added separately to add colour evenly throughout the decoration. Artificial berries can be used if real ones are not available.

To make this splendid Christmas centrepiece, take a flat circular base such as a cake board and glue a cone of florists' foam to the centre. Then glue or staple a length of gold netting round the edge of the base, gathering it into bunches as you go. Crumple lengths of red fabric or ribbon into double loops and wire the ends. Arrange them in a ring on top of the gold.

Spray a number of Chinese lanterns and lotus seedheads with gold paint. When they are dry, wire the ends and insert them evenly spaced into the cone. Intersperse several long-eared pods throughout, pushing · them deep into the arrangement. Add highlights with a few honesty seedheads (silver dollar plant). Then wire together bunches of small red helichrysum (strawflower or everlasting) and dot them among the other plants, adding colour throughout. Finish off by inserting a few groups of white leaf skeletons — about two to three leaves per group.

A pair of candlestick holders is transformed by a tightly-packed arrangement of dried flowers. For each stick, cut a sphere of florist's foam in half and hollow out the centre of each piece so that the foam sits snugly round the stem. Wrap a piece of florists' tape around the two halves to hold them together.

Push short stems of orange South African daisy (a form of helichrysum) into the foam, keeping the arrangement spherical. Then fill in with small wired clumps of red helichrysum (strawflower or everlasting) and pink miniature sunray, being sure not to leave any gaps.

Create some pretty coasters using a few flowers and some mother-of-pearl discs. The latter can be bought from any shop specializing in shells. They should measure at least 4cm (1½in) more than the diameter of your glass base. Choose any combination of flowers or seedheads — shown above are helichrysum, honesty and hydrangea. Cut the heads off the plants.

Now create a ring around the edge of a shell by gluing the heads in position. The honesty can be stuck down first — the heads slightly overlapping — and the red helichrysum can be glued down on top at regular intervals. If you are only using helichrysum, alternate the colours for a more interesting effect.

An old topper, bursting with colour, makes a delightfully unconventional design for the festive season. Begin by putting a large brick of soaked florists' foam into a container which will fit comfortably into the hat. Fan out sprays of *Mallalika* foliage and fill in with September flowers (a form of aster).

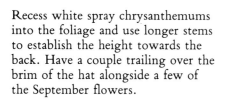

Rich red holly berries add a brilliant splash of colour to this attractive festive arrangement. Choose a long shallow glass bowl and pack it with wire mesh. Crushed wire mesh is the best medium for this type of shallow bowl as it keeps the flowers from sagging.

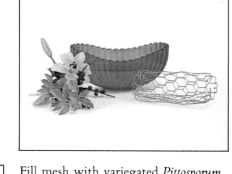

Recess white spray chrysanthemums into the foliage and use longer stems to establish the height towards the back. Have a couple trailing over the brim of the hat alongside a few of the September flowers.

Fill mesh with variegated *Pittosporum,* a bushy foliage which maintains its fullness even when cut short. Stems of gypsophilia (also known as baby's breath in the United States) are added next, spread across the arrangement.

The focal point of the arrangement is poinsettia flowers which should be conditioned first by searing the stem ends with a lighted candle. fill in the outline and balance the display with deep red spray carnations.

The three main stems of yellow lily, straddling the length of the vase, form the focal point. Intersperse the whole display with holly (known more specifically as English holly in the United States) berries, retaining the longer twigs for contrast and balance.

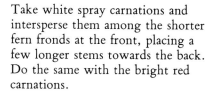

Keep the champagne in the refrigerator this Christmas and use the ice bucket for red roses instead! First, put soaked florists' foam at the base of the bucket. Then insert some variegated foliage — shown here is a spineless form of holly. Intersperse this with eight or nine red roses, still in bud. Have two or three longer stems rising from the foliage to one side at the back.

Here, a wicker waste-paper basket forms the basis of an attractive festive arrangement of ferns and carnations. If you don't have a suitable red basket, you can spray a natural coloured one with red paint. Begin by taping soaked florists' foam into a container and positioning it inside the basket. Then fan out the fern fronds to form the setting for the flowers.

Take white spray carnations and intersperse them among the shorter fern fronds at the front, placing a few longer stems towards the back. Do the same with the bright red carnations.

Fill in all the available space with jonquil, following the outline. The gold is highlighted by the yellow-edged foliage. (A handy tip: the roses will last longer if the stems are placed in boiling water for a minute before being given a long drink.)

Finish off by adding a sprinkling of September flowers (a form of aster) to soften the whole effect. (This display can also be acheived by pushing tiny phials of flowers into the soil of a real fern, such an arrangement being known as a pot-et-fleurs.

A silver bowl bursting with roses and freesias makes the perfect centrepiece for the festive season. Fill the bowl with water. Then cut short the stems of the cream spider chrysanthemums (to around 5cm, 2in) and pack into the bowl's wire mesh centre – these will give depth to the final arrangement.

Place yellow roses in between the chrysanthemums, keeping the stems slightly longer. Next, intersperse the arrangement with a few freesias.

Finally, place *Leucodendron* and freesia buds among the display, ensuring the stems are slightly longer than those of the other flowers; these will provide a stark contrast to the gold and silver. For a short period of time, such as during a dinner party, a full blown rose at the foot of the bowl will complete the picture, though, out of the water, the bloom's lifespan will be limited.

Bring your table to life with this attractive floral candle ring. Stick double-sided tape around the outside edge of a sponge ring mould. Adhere pleated green cellophane to this and secure with a little more sticky tape. This creates an attractive trim and is an alternative to foliage.

Insert chunks of soaked florists' foam into the ring, placing slightly thicker pieces at the back. Working around the ring insert short stems of daisy chrysanthemums to complete the circle.

Throughout the chrysanthemums dot blue-dyed yarrow and some little gold-sprayed cones on wires. Three white candles complete the garland. (The non-drip variety are best for a floral arrangement.)

This sumptuous arrangement of plump flowers on a green glass cake stand looks almost edible! Place a round piece of soaked florists' foam in the centre of the stand. Then use yellow roses and alstroemeria alternately, cutting the stems on a slant and keeping them short so that once inserted into the foam the flower heads rest on the edge of the dish.

Finally, top the arrangement with a few sprays of mimosa which will retain its pretty fluffy heads longer if conditioned first. This is done by submerging flower heads under cold water then dipping stems into 2.5cm (1in) of boiling water for a few seconds. Stand in a jug of warm water until the flowers have dried off.

The next layer comprises the bobbly 'flowers' of *Leucodendron brunia* followed by a ring of Persian buttercups. The latter will last longer if their stems are put into boiling water for a few seconds, before being given a long drink.

A shallow ovenware dish forms the base for this arrangement of fiery chrysanthemums, carnations and capsicums (appropriately known as Christmas pepper in the United States). Place soaked florists' foam into the dish and cover with *Viburnum tinus* allowing the stems to escape over the sides of the dish.

To create the focal point of the arrangement, take six full blooming orange carnations and arrange them uniformly across the outline.

Fill in the outline with greenish white spray chrysanthemums. Their colour provides a dramatic contrast to the orange carnations, and their flame-shaped petals aptly fit the theme of the arrangement. Complete the display with capsicums, taking them through and along the length of the arrangement.

Add richness and colour to the home during the festive season with this vibrant design. First, roll some wire mesh into a tube, pack it with dry moss and close the ends. Squash the base into the basket and wire it in place as shown. Begin to form the outline of the arrangement with bleached white helichrysum (strawflower or everlasting), creating a dome shape.

Continue to build up the shape with white proteus. Add some clubrush next, followed by a number of cones, such as these meridianum. The colour of these two plants cleverly picks up the brown in the basket.

Wood always provides a perfect setting for dried flowers, and an old wooden plane makes an unusual festive design. Cut a block of florists' foam and wedge it tightly into the hole. Arrange wired clumps of cluster-flowered sunray first, keeping the outline low. Follow with pink *Leucodendron brunia,* allowing it to break out of the shape and dangle low over the sides.

Now add interest and a dash of colour with a few stems of bottlebrush. Put them in singly and keep them short so that their rich colour lies deep within the arrangement.

Complete the display with bright yellow clumps of cressia and cluster-flowered helichrysum. Place them low down in the arrangement, filling in the gaps between the other plants.

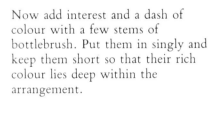

Soften the effect with a few clumps of grass interspersed throughout. To finish, add contrasting texture with three or four heads of *Leucodendron plumosum* set deep into the display.

To make a change from the more traditional holly, decorate your picture frames with this stunning tartan design. Cut a slice of florists' foam to fit one corner of the frame and tape it in place. Begin to loosely build up the shape using single stems of clubrush.

Add a splash of colour throughout the display with bright yellow cressia, allowing some to trail across the frame and picture. Then insert a number of single stems of bottlebrush to add interest and colour.

Fill out the display with plenty of bottlebrush foliage. Then add highlights with a few white leaf skeletons such as these peepal leaves.

Finally, make a double bow out of tartan ribbon, wiring it together rather than tying it. Attach this to the lower portion of the arrangement so that the long tails of the bow trail across the frame. Repeat the whole procedure on the opposite corner, being sure to keep the design well balanced.

The framework of this seasonal garland is made of cones and walnuts. Wire the cones by wrapping stub wire around the base. For the walnuts, push stub wire through one end as far as it will go. Take a group of cones and nuts and twist the wires together. Add to the base of the group and twist the wires again to secure. Continue in this way until the garland is long enough.

These miniature arrangements make pretty novelties to hang on the Christmas tree. One of them is made with cinnamon sticks. Take about three sticks and bind them together with wire. Wire on a double bow made out of gold gift wrap ribbon and then add a posy of cones and small red helichrysum (strawflower or everlasting).

Wire together a double bow made from gold gift wrap ribbon and wire two extra tails on to it. (Just fold a length of ribbon in half for the tails and wire in the middle.) Attach the bow to one end of the garland, then wire a long length of ribbon to the same end. Wrap this through the garland, twisting it round the cones. Leave a long tail at the far end.

To make the other arrangement, first spray a small basket and some walnuts with gold paint. When these are dry, fill the basket with a block of florists' foam. Pack the foam with gold coloured South African daisies (a type of helichrysum) to form a spherical shape.

To finish, wire together small groups of bright Chinese lanterns and bunches of quaking grass. Intersperse them amongst the cones, entangling the wires to secure them.

Push a length of wire through one end of each of the walnuts. Insert three or four nuts into the display, pushing them deep down amongst the flowers. Wire a small bow and attach it to the handle. Finally, hang each arrangement by means of a loop of gold cord.

H ere are two more colourful decorations to hang on the Christmas tree. For the red ball, take a length of cord and wire the ends together, forming a loop. Push the wire right the way through a sphere of florists' foam and double it back on itself — into the foam — to secure. Now cover the foam with flowers.

Pack the flowers tightly into the foam to maintain the spherical shape. Those used here are deep red helichrysum (strawflower or everlasting). Fill in with little clumps of red nipplewort (or broom bloom). To finish, gather up and wire small pieces of silver netting, then insert them amongst the flowers.

T his pretty display, arranged in a tiny gift box, makes an attractive miniature decoration. It would also make a delightful present. And with all that lavender, it smells as lovely as it looks. First cut a small block of florists' foam and pop it inside the box. Then wire a couple of red ribbons into bows.

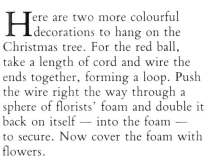

For this design wire together a few flowers, such as these small white helichrysum and blue-dyed *Leucodendron brunia,* and attach three decorative bells. Gather up a piece of red netting and bind it on to the flowers. Make a double red bow, tie a long piece of ribbon round the middle (by which to hang the decoration) and attach the bow to the netting with wire.

Wire together bunches of lavender and pack them into the foam, keeping the arrangement tallest in the middle and splaying it out at the sides. Now scatter tiny, daisy-like glixia or grass daisies throughout; push some deep into the display. Finish off by attaching the two red bows, one to the box, the other higher up on a stem of lavender.

A beautifully wrapped gift is a pleasure to give and a pleasure to receive. So here are over 40 imaginative ways to make your Christmas presents look that extra bit special. Having been shown how to wrap a variety of shapes, you will find some simple ways to make your own wrapping paper — a great cost saver — and lots of pretty decorations such as ribbon ties, rosettes and pom-poms to add those all-important finishing touches. There are also some ingenious ideas for greetings cards that are both simple to make and effective, and, finally, lots of inexpensive ways to make your own gift tags using last year's cards or motifs cut from wrapping paper.

Sometimes the gift wrap seems almost as expensive as the gift itself. But there are plenty of ways to get stylish results without the expense. Reels of gift ribbon can be turned into a vast array of different decorations, from stunning rosettes you couldn't tell apart from shop-bought versions to pretty pom-poms and posies. Braid, cord and even candies can also be used to make gifts that extra bit special.

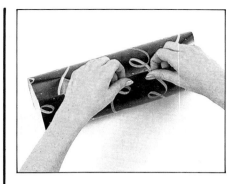

When wrapping a cylinder, avoid using very thick or textured paper as it will be difficult to fold neatly. Cut the paper longer than the cylinder, allowing for extra paper at each end to cover half the cylinder's diameter, and just wider than the gift's circumference. Roll the paper around the parcel and secure with a little tape.

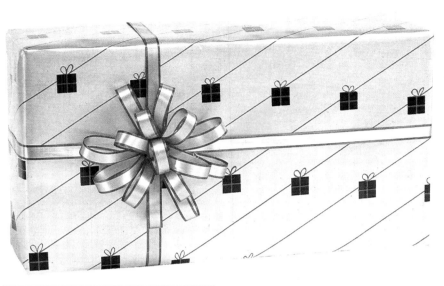

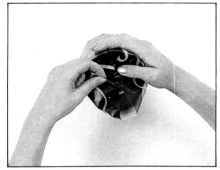

Begin folding the ends of the paper in a series of small triangles as shown here. Continue around the whole circumference, making sure that the 'triangles' are neatly folded into the centre.

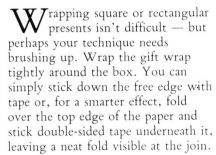

Wrapping square or rectangular presents isn't difficult — but perhaps your technique needs brushing up. Wrap the gift wrap tightly around the box. You can simply stick down the free edge with tape or, for a smarter effect, fold over the top edge of the paper and stick double-sided tape underneath it, leaving a neat fold visible at the join.

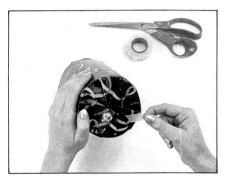

Use a single piece of tape at the centre to fix all the folds in place. If the finished folds are not even, you could cheat a little by sticking a circle of matching gift wrap over each end of the cylinder.

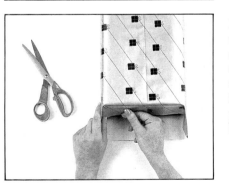

If your paper has a linear design, try to align the design so that the join is not too obvious. Fold the joined section of paper down over the end of the box to make a flap; crease the fold neatly. Trim off any excess paper so there is no unnecessary bulk.

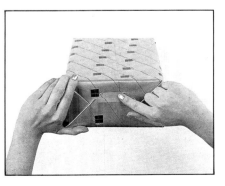

Crease the side flaps firmly, and fold them over the ends of the gift. Smoothing your hand along the side of the box and round on to the end ensures that each flap fits tightly. Fold up the remaining triangular flap, pulling it firmly along the edge of the box, and stick down; use invisible tape (its matt surface is scarcely discernible) or double-sided for the best results.

The usual method of wrapping a sphere is to gather the paper around the gift and bunch it all together at the top. Here is a more stylish method. Put your circular gift in the centre of a square of paper, checking that the two sides of paper just meet at the top when wrapped around the gift. Cut off the corners of the square to form a circle of paper.

Bring one section of the paper to the top of the gift and begin to pleat it to fit the object as shown. The paper pleats at the top of the gift will end up at more or less the same point; hold them in place every three or four pleats with a tiny piece of sticky tape.

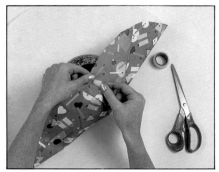

Continue pleating neatly and tightly all the way round the circle. It isn't as complicated or as time-consuming as it sounds once you've got the knack! When you have finished, the pile of pleats on top of the gift should look small and neat. Then you can either cover them with a small circle of paper stuck in place or, more attractively, add a bunch of colourful ribbons.

Wrapping awkwardly-shaped presents is just that — awkward. The gift wrap always looks creased and untidy around the angles of the gift. The solution is not to use paper — instead, use brightly-coloured cellophane which doesn't crumple. Cut a square of cellophane a great deal larger than your gift.

Gather the cellophane up and tie it into a bunch above the present. Fan out the excess and add some curled ribbon as a finishing touch. Alternatively, if your gift is cylindrical, roll it in cellophane somewhat longer than the parcel and gather the ends with ribbon.

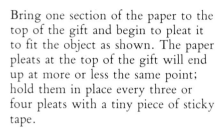

Glittering wrapping paper is always glamorous, and with glitter available in such a variety of colours your creativity need know no bounds! Spread out a sheet of plain coloured paper and, using a bottle of glue with a fine nozzle, draw a series of simple patterns across it.

Wallpaper is often useful as a gift covering — particularly if your present is very large. Here we have used thick wallpaper with an embossed pattern and given it a touch of style and individuality. Wrap your gift, and choose some wax crayons in contrasting shades. Rub a colour over the raised surface of the wallpaper to highlight one of the motifs in the design.

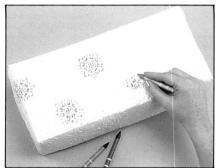

Sprinkle a line of glitter across the paper. Tip up the sheet and gently shake all the glitter from one side of the paper to the other, across the glued designs, making sure that all the patterns have been well covered. Tip the excess glitter off the page on to a sheet of newspaper; the glitter can then be used again.

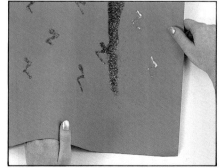

Choose another colour, and use it to pick out another section in the pattern. (Instead of wax crayons, you could use coloured pencils or chalk; the latter would need to be rubbed with a tissue afterwards to remove loose dust. The medium you choose must slide over the embossing without colouring in the whole design — paint is therefore not suitable.)

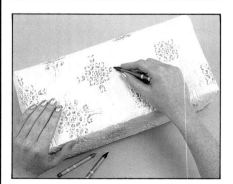

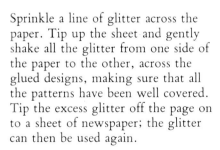

Now use the glue to make more designs and coat these in glitter of a different colour. Localize the sprinkling of the glitter over the new patterns to be covered and leave to dry. Tip off the excess glitter and return it to its container.

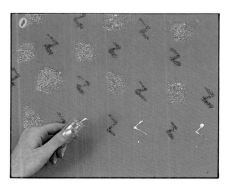

Repeat the process using a third colour and continue with as many shades as you like. A tip while wrapping your gift — you'll probably find that ordinary tape will not stick to the surface of wallpaper; double-sided tape used between two folds will be more effective.

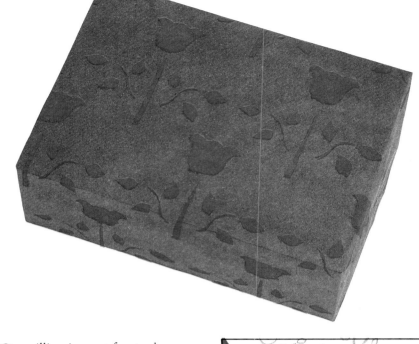

All kinds of effects can be achieved with a sponge and some paint. You'll need a piece of natural sponge as man-made sponge doesn't produce the right effect. Choose some plain paper and mix up some poster paint to a fairly runny consistency. Test the paint on a spare piece of paper until you're happy with the colour.

Stencilling is great fun to do — and so easy. Design a simple motif then make a trace of it. With a soft pencil, scribble over the back of the trace and put the tracing paper face up on stencil cardboard. Draw round the design again, pressing hard so that the lines are transferred on to the cardboard beneath. Repeat the motif several times and cut out the shapes with a craft knife.

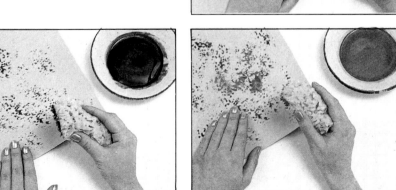

Dab the sponge into the paint and pat it evenly over the paper. The sponge should hold sufficient paint for about four 'dabs' before you need to dip it into the paint again. You'll need to mix up a lot of paint as the sponge absorbs a considerable amount.

Rinse the sponge out well and squeeze dry. When the paper has dried, repeat the process with another colour — you can use as many colours as you wish. Match the ribbon to one of the colours; see page 49 for instructions on how to create the ribbon trim shown here.

Position the cut-out stencil on plain paper, and either hold it or use masking tape to keep it in place. Mix up some poster paint, keeping the consistency quite thick. Apply the paint through the stencil, using a stiff brush. When you have finished a row of motifs, lift the stencil carefully and blot it on newspaper so that it is ready to use again. Leave the design to dry.

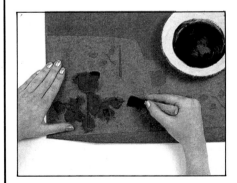

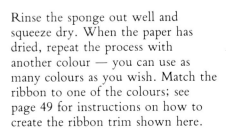

Keep repeating the process until you have covered enough paper to wrap your gift. To help you keep the spacing even between each run of motifs, add some 'markers' to the stencil. Cut half a motif at the end of the run and another one above the run to mark the position of the next row. Paint the markers along with the other motifs, then use this image for re-positioning the next row.

Employ a humble potato to create simple yet beautiful designs. Begin by cutting a large potato in half and draw a simple design on it. Use a sharp knife or craft knife to sculp the potato, leaving the design raised from the surface.

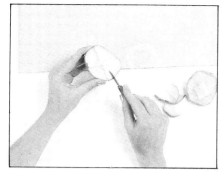

To ensure a regular print, draw a grid lightly in pencil on a sheet of plain paper. Then mix up fairly thick poster paint and apply it to the potato-cut with a paintbrush. Print the design in the middle of each square of the grid. You should be able to do two or three prints before the colour fades and needs replenishing.

Stylish, expensive-looking wrapping paper can be achieved very quickly with this method of spray stencilling. Choose some plain coloured paper for a base, and make your stencils from plain cardboard or paper. Cut the stencils into squares of two different sizes; alternatively you could use any kind of basic shape — stars, circles or whatever.

Cover the whole sheet with one design. Cut another design on another potato half; repeat the whole process, this time printing on the cross of the grid. When the paint is thoroughly dry, rub out the grid lines still visible and wrap up your present.

Lay some of the shapes in a random pattern across the plain paper, holding them in place with a spot of Plasticine or modelling clay. Cover the whole paper with paint spray. Use car paint or craft spray paint, but do carry it out in a well-ventilated room.

Once the paint is dry take off the sprayed squares and put a new random pattern of fresh squares across the paper. Overlap some of the original squares with the new ones to create interesting effects, then spray the entire sheet with a second colour of paint. Remove the squares and leave the wrapping paper to dry before using it.

DELICATE DOILIES

GET IT TAPED

The delicate silhouette of a doily against a contrasting background colour looks attractive on a gift. Wrap your present up in plain paper and glue the doilies wherever you like. To decorate the corners of a large gift, fold a doily in half, then in half again.

Unfold the doily carefully and spread it out. Cut off one of the quarters of the doily; the folds along which you should cut will be clearly visible.

Paste the doily over one corner of the gift as shown. Repeat with alternate corners, unless your gift has enough space to take a doily over each corner without overlap. The doilies don't have to be white: silver or gold is also effective. Nor do they have to be circular — square ones would be smart on a square-sided present.

Brightly-coloured adhesive tape can give any plain wrapping paper a touch of style. A geometric design is easiest to create with tape, and the most effective; curves are rather difficult! Work out your design first and measure it out accurately on the parcel in pencil.

Stick the tapes in place along the pencil marks. Take care that the tapes don't stretch at all during application or they will cause the paper to pucker slightly. Sticky tapes are available in an enormous variety of colours, textures and patterns; choose a strong contrast with your paper.

Y ou couldn't distinguish this pointed pom-pom from a shop-bought version — yet it's a fraction of the price! Use ribbon which sticks to itself when moistened. Make a small loop by wrapping the ribbon round your thumb; moisten the ribbon and fix it in place. Now twist the ribbon back on itself to form a pointed loop, as shown; stick it in position.

Go on looping the ribbon in twists, spacing them evenly as you go. It is fairly fiddly but keep trying — you'll soon master the technique. You'll probably need to wait a minute between each fixing for the ribbon's glue to dry before turning the next loop.

I t's hard to believe that these pretty flowers and the butterfly are made from tights (pantyhose) and fuse wire. Cut up a pair of discarded tights or stockings. Cut some 15 amp fuse wire into lengths, some shorter than others, suitable for making petals. Make a circular shape out of each length and twist the ends together.

Continue winding outwards in a circle until the bow is as big as you want; cut off the ribbon, leaving a small tail just visible. Attach the pom-pom to the present with double-sided tape.

Put a piece of stocking material over a wire circle and pull it tight, making sure that the whole circle is covered. Fix it in position by firmly winding matching cotton around the twisted stem of the wire. Cut off the excess fabric.

Take seven petals, smaller ones in the centre, and bind them all tightly with thread. Bend the petals around until you're happy with the look of the flower. Tie up your parcel with ribbon and attach the flower with double-sided tape. The butterfly is made in just the same way: two pairs of 'petals' are bound together with thread, then bent into the shape of wings.

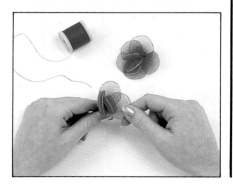

CHRISTMAS LEAVES

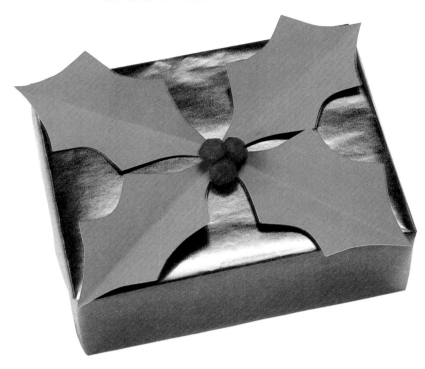

DING DONG MERRILY

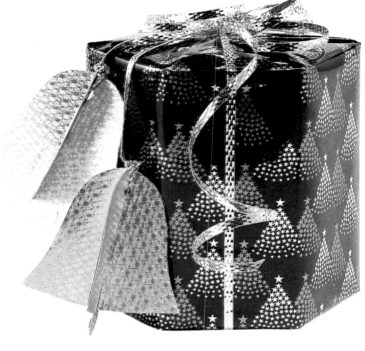

Holly leaves are an attractive shape and perfect for decorating a festive gift. Measure the length of the diagonal across the top of your parcel. On a sheet of plain paper, draw a large holly leaf, the 'vein' of which measures slightly more than half the length of the diagonal.

Trace four holly leaves on to some green cardboard, using the template you have just created. Cut the leaves out and bend them in the middle; creasing them slightly where the central vein would be.

Make the berries from a ball of cotton wool (known as absorbent cotton in the United States) wrapped in two squares of red tissue paper. Put a dab of glue inside and twist up the tissue tightly at the base. When the glue is dry, cut off as much excess of the twist as possible. Group the leaves and berries on the parcel; attach with glue or double-sided tape.

These Christmas bells ring out gaily from your present. Make two paper templates, both bell-shaped, with one showing the outline of the clapper from the bottom edge. From thin cardboard, cut out two of each shape.

Cover all the cardboard shapes with gold paper (or any colour which would co-ordinate with your wrapping paper). Cover both sides, and trim away all the excess paper. On the bell shapes with the clapper, cut a slit from the curved top of the bell to the centre of the bell. On the others (the plain ones) cut a slit from the middle of the bottom edge, also to the centre.

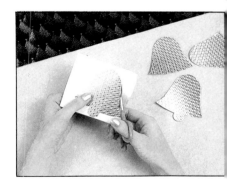

Pierce a hole in the top of the plain bell shapes and thread them with a length of ribbon. Then slot the pairs of bell shapes together (i.e. the plain one, and the one with the clapper) so that they form three-dimensional shapes, as shown here. Tie a group of as many bells as you like on to your gift.

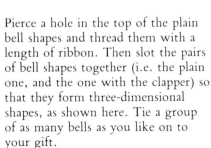

ELIZABETHAN BOW

FLOPPY BOW

The scrolled shapes of this decoration are reminiscent of the curlicues embellishing Queen Elizabeth I's signature. Wrap up your present, and choose some gift wrapping ribbon to match or contrast with the colours of the gift wrap. Hold the end of the ribbon in one hand, and form a loop as shown, leaving a small tail.

Make a corresponding loop below, forming a figure-of-eight shape. This will be the size of the finished product; adjust the proportion of the loops at this stage if you want a bigger or smaller bow. Continue folding loops of the same size until you have as many as you want — seven at each end is usually enough.

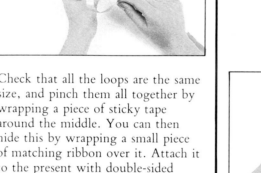

Check that all the loops are the same size, and pinch them all together by wrapping a piece of sticky tape around the middle. You can then hide this by wrapping a small piece of matching ribbon over it. Attach it to the present with double-sided tape.

This bow, with its floppy loops, gives a soft, casual effect. You'll need about 2m (6ft) of acetate or craft ribbon, 2.5cm (1in) wide. Cut off about 30cm (12in) ribbon; wind the rest round your fingers. Holding the ribbon firmly, make a notch in both edges with a pair of scissors as shown, cutting through all the layers of ribbon.

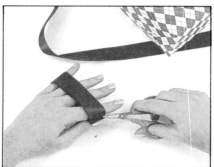

Take the ribbon off your hand and notch the edges of the opposite side of the loops. Flatten the loops so that the notches match in the centre and loops are formed either side. Take the 30cm (12in) length of ribbon and tie it tightly around the notches as shown.

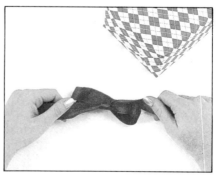

Starting with the innermost loop on one side of the folded bow, gently pull each loop away from the other loops and into the centre of the bow. You'll end up with each loop being visible, thus forming the shape of the finished rosette.

A pom-pom bow adds a cheerful touch to a present of any shape or size. Use the kind of ribbon which will stick to itself when moistened. Cut seven strips; four measuring about 30cm (12in), the other three about 23cm (9in). You'll also need a small piece of ribbon about 5cm (2in), for the central loop.

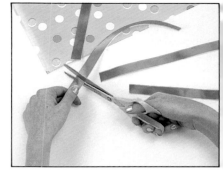

Overlap the ends of each of the long strips and moisten them; stick them together to form a loop. Moisten the centre of each loop and stick it together as shown. Cross two of the looped strips, joining them at the central point. Repeat with the other two loops. Join both crosses together so the loops are evenly spaced apart.

H ere is an easy way to achieve a very pretty effect. Choose three colours of narrow ribbon which co-ordinate with your gift wrap. Using one ribbon, tie it around your parcel in the usual way, crossing it underneath the parcel and knotting it tightly on top; leave long ends. Tie a length of different coloured ribbon to the centre point, then do the same with a third colour.

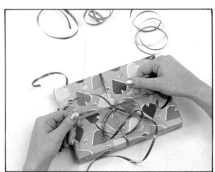

Continue tying on lengths of ribbon so that you end up with two lengths, (that is, four ends) of each colour. Tie the central knots tightly to keep them as small as possible. Pull a ribbon length gently along the open blade of a pair of scissors; this will cause it to curl into ringlets. Repeat with each length until they are as curly as you want.

Loop the three shorter lengths, and cross them over each other, fixing them together at the centre. Stick the resulting star in the middle of the large rosette. Fill in the centre with the tiny loop. Obviously, the length and width of ribbon can be varied, according to the size you want the finished pom-pom to be.

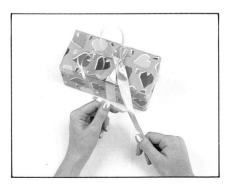

An alternative is to use wide gift ribbon. Tie it round the parcel once, making sure that the knot is as neat as possible and leaving long ends. Cut two small nicks in the ribbon, dividing it evenly into three; pull it to split the ribbon up to the knot. Run each of these lengths along the blade of a pair of scissors until they form ringlets.

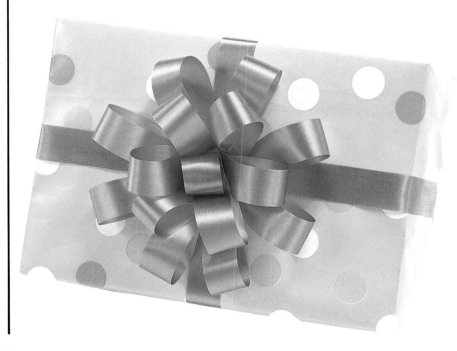

A sweet treat for children of all ages! Boiled sweets (hard candies) with plain cellophane wrappers look best because of their clear colours, but you can use alternatives such as toffees or peppermints. Select five or six of the chosen sweets, and hold them in a bunch by one end of their wrappers.

Take a narrow piece of ribbon and tie all the sweets together tightly; if the wrappers are a little short it may help to bind them first with sewing thread. Leave a reasonably long piece of ribbon on each side of the bunch of sweets so that you can attach it easily to the parcel.

Tie the same ribbon around the parcel, leaving the ends long, then tie the sweets to the centre point as shown. Curl up each ribbon end by pulling it gently along the open blade of a pair of scissors. Try to co-ordinate your gift wrap with the chosen confectionery — black and white paper with humbugs, for example, would look very attractive.

Brightly-coloured drinking straws lend themselves to decorating presents. Look for colours to co-ordinate with your gift wrap. The straws can be made of paper or plastic; both work well. Select the colours you want and cut four straws in half; discard one of each half. Cut another four straws in two, leaving one section slightly longer than the other; retain both pieces.

Place four halves, one of each colour, together over a central point in a star shape and staple them together. Do the same with the other slightly longer straws and their shorter counterparts so that you end up with three stars of slightly different sizes. With the smallest on top and largest on the bottom, staple all three together. Attach the triple star to the parcel with double-sided tape.

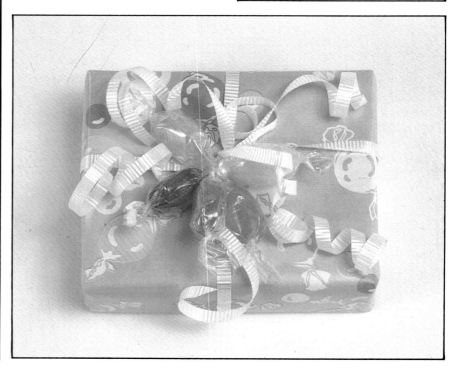

Craft foil is the perfect material for creating this decoration. Use a compass to draw four circles; the ones shown here measure 8cm (3in), 6.5cm (2½in) 5cm (2in) and 4cm (1½in) in diameter. Draw an inner ring of 2cm (¾in) in the centre of each circle. Rule lines to divide the circles evenly into eighths; cut along the lines to the inner circle to make eight segments.

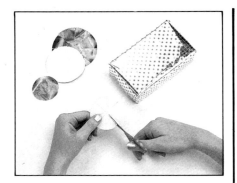

Roll each segment of the circle into a cone; use a dab of glue to secure it. Make sure that each cone shape has a good sharp point by rolling it fairly tightly. The process is a bit fiddly; you may find it easier to roll each cone around the point of a stencil to give it shape. Repeat with the other circles.

Starting with the largest star shape, glue all the stars inside each other, positioning the points of each star between those of the preceding ones. When the glue is dry, gently bend each cone of the middle two stars towards the centre, to fill in the central space, so forming a semi-circular three-dimensional star.

A pretty arrangement of dried flowers make a lovely decoration for a gift. You can pick grasses and seedheads in the country or you can dry flowers from your own garden; it's fun and quite easy. Or you can buy them, though of course it's more expensive that way! First cut the dried plants all the same length.

Bunch the flowers together; when you're happy with them, wrap sticky tape around the stalks. Hide the tape by winding ribbon over it. Tie ribbon round the parcel, finish off with a knot, and attach the little bouquet by tying its trailing ribbons over the knot; trim the ends of the bouquet ribbon away. Using the ends of the other ribbon, finish off by making a pretty bow over the bouquet.

ROSEBUDS

RIBBON ROSETTES

A small posy of pretty rosebuds makes a very special decoration for an extra-special gift. Cut a small length of ribbon — about 6-9cm (2-3½in), depending on the width of ribbon you've chosen. Fold the ribbon in half, right sides together, and join the two ends with a small seam. Run a gathering thread around one edge.

Pull the gathering thread tight to form the rosebud; sew it firmly across the base. Make another two or three buds and sew them all together at the base; you may need to add the occasional supporting stitch at the top edges to hold the buds close together.

The leaves add an attractive contrast. They are made from a strip of green ribbon, two corners of which have been folded over to form a point. Fix with double-sided tape since glue can leave a mark on ribbon. The illustration below shows the rosebuds grouped on a length of ribbon twice the width of the flowers, set off with narrow green ribbon.

A winning idea for any gift! Cut a length of fairly wide ribbon; you'll need about 30cm (12in) for each rosette. Fold it in half with the right sides of the ribbon together; sew up the two ends to form a seam.

Using tiny stitches, gather up one edge of the ribbon. Pull the gathering thread tight, arranging the rosette into a neat circle as you do so. Finish it off by sewing across the base. Make as many rosettes as you need and attach them to your parcel with double-sided tape.

A fan adds panache to a plain giftbox. Cut one long edge from a large rectangular paper doily, making it about 7cm (2 3/4in) deep. Cut cartridge paper a little deeper and wider than this and cover with foil gift wrap using spray adhesive. Glue the doily strip to one side. Cut the top edge following the curves of the doily, then pleat up concertina style.

Paint-sprayed plastic holly adds a flourish to a plain box. Spray two sprigs of holly with silver then, when dry, spray lightly with bronze to highlight the leaves and berries. Wire the holly together, then wire on three small glass balls, chosen to colour match the gift wrap. Wrap a piece of double-sided tape around the stems and wrap with silver crepe paper, gluing the end down.

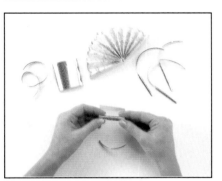

Open out the concertina into a fan shape and run a length of double-sided tape along the base to hold it in place. Do not remove the backing paper. From narrow curling ribbon cut five 15cm (6in) lengths, and from foil, five 6cm (2 1/2in) squares. Stick a square to the end of each ribbon with double-sided tape and curl the foil around it. Secure the end with more tape.

To make the bow, cut a strip of silver crepe paper along the length of the roll, 74cm (29in) long and 12.5 (5in) wide. Fold in the two long edges to overlap and crimp the folded edges between your fingers, gently stretching the paper. Pinch into a bow shape and wrap a short length of crepe paper, raw edges tucked in, around the centre. Secure with double-sided tape.

Remove the backing paper from the base of the fan and stick the ribbon ends to the centre. Make a gift tag from a rectangle of paper and cover with foil using spray adhesive. Punch a hole in it, attach a length of gold thread and join to the fan. Curl the ends of three lengths of ribbon and stick them to the front of the fan with PVA glue or tape. Stick the fan diagonally across the giftbox.

Cut a 6.5cm (2 1/2in) wide strip of crepe paper along the length of the roll as before, cutting enough to wrap around the giftbox in both directions. Crimp the edges and attach to the box with double-sided tape, placing the joins under the box. Press a double-sided adhesive pad to the centre cross of the ties and press the holly bouquet in place. Finally, stick the bow in place over the holly.

GIFT BOX ROSETTE

TISSUE TWISTS

Y ou will need the type of gift wrap ribbon which sticks to itself when moistened for this decoration. First cut two strips of ribbon at least 40cm (16in) long. Twist each piece into a figure-of-eight, moistening the ends to hold in place. Stick one piece at right angles over the other. Repeat with two more strips 5cm (2in) shorter.

Stick the second rosette on top of the first. To finish, make a loop out of a short strip of ribbon and stick it in the centre. For a more traditional rosette, simply make the loops shorter and tighter.

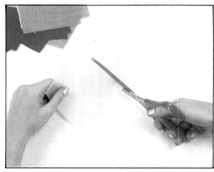

Y ou can make these decorations in a single colour, but they look more effective if you choose several. For each twist, you need three squares of tissue for the outer colour, two for the middle colour and two for the inner (most visible) section. The squares needed for the inner section are smaller than those for the outside; the middle leaves must be of a size in between.

Pick up the squares in order, putting one on top of the other; outer colour first, then the middle, then the inner squares. Position them so that the corners of each square are at a different angle, as shown. Put a couple of stitches through the centre point to secure all the squares together and leave some thread hanging.

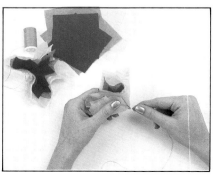

Fold the whole thing in half and half again, twisting the folded point at the base to form the shape of the 'flower'. Pull the thread out at the point, and wind it tightly around the twisted base to secure it; 'fluff' out the finished decoration. Make several 'flowers' and group them together on your present.

A delicate posy of dried flowers provides a perfect decoration for any gift. Choose a selection of brightly coloured, small-headed flowers and tie them together with fine wire. The flowers used here are blue larkspur, yellow South African daisy, (a type of helichrysum), small red roses and a touch of golden rod. Wrap a strip of white ribbon around the stems and finish off with a bow.

The posy on this gift box is made up in a similar way, using flowers in a range of colours that match those of the box. The posy contains green amaranthus (love-lies-bleeding), mauve xeranthemums, pink gypsophila (baby's breath), blue larkspur, cream 'cauliflower' and yellow dudinea.

Attach the posies to the gifts with glue. Alternatively you can wire them on. To do this you will need to pierce two small holes in the side of the box. Wrap wire round the stems of the posy and thread it through the holes; secure on the inside.

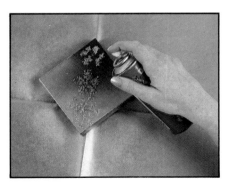

This is a simple but elegant way to use empty gift boxes as containers for pot-pourri. We have selected a green and a black box. Take the lid off one of the boxes and lightly secure three whole flower heads of cow parsley diagonally across it. With aerosol spray paint, give the top of the box two light coats of gold paint.

When the paint is dry, remove the parsley to reveal the unsprayed part of the box. This shows up as a pretty pattern through the paint. Now fix the gold sprayed cow parsley to the other box lid. These boxes are filled with 'Noel' pot-pourri, which is a festive mixture of small cones, tree bark and citrus peel. Cover the pot-pourri with cling film (plastic wrap) before replacing the lids.

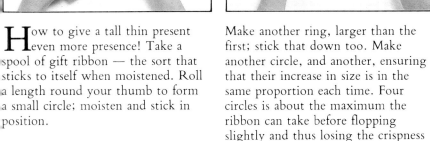

How to give a tall thin present even more presence! Take a spool of gift ribbon — the sort that sticks to itself when moistened. Roll a length round your thumb to form a small circle; moisten and stick in position.

Make another ring, larger than the first; stick that down too. Make another circle, and another, ensuring that their increase in size is in the same proportion each time. Four circles is about the maximum the ribbon can take before flopping slightly and thus losing the crispness of the decoration.

It is quite easy to paint wide ribbon to co-ordinate with your wrapping paper. And the results are stunning! Choose a gift wrap with a simple design. Decide whether you want the ribbon to be a positive version of the paper's design, like the blue example shown here, or a negative one, like the black and white suggestions. Experiment with poster paint on your chosen ribbon.

Keep the design very simple and stylized. When you're happy with your pattern, paint enough ribbon to wrap up the gift, allowing sufficient for a fairly large bow. Leave the ribbon to dry thoroughly before tying it around the parcel. If the paint does crack a little when tying up the ribbon, simply touch it up and leave it to dry again.

The metallic sheen of sequins, and the strip of metallic plastic from which they are pressed, looks rather chic. Sequin waste — that is, the strip of metallic plastic — can be bought by the metre or yard from good craft shops. This idea looks best on rectangular flat parcels. Wrap a piece of sequin waste around the length of the present; fix it with tape.

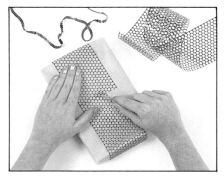

Take another strip of sequin waste and join the two ends to make a large loop. Use sticky tape to fix them, making sure the holes overlap so that the join is almost invisible.

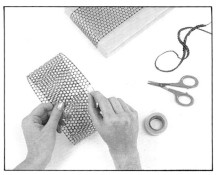

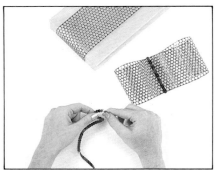

Put a strip of threaded sequin trim of the same colour across the middle of the loop. Remove a few loose sequins so that you can tie the trim in position. Repeat with another length of trim; space the two evenly apart in the centre of the loop to form a bow. Attach the bow to the parcel with double-sided tape. Sequin trim as a gift tie in its own right gives a glamorous finish to any gift.

This decoration looks best on a rectangular gift. Take 66cm (26in) of woven ribbon; lay it flat. Measure 13cm (5in) from one end of the ribbon and mark both edges. Then mark along the ribbon's length a further 10cm (4in), 7.5cm (3in), 5cm (2in), 7.5cm (3in), 10cm (4in). Using one piece of thread, pick up tiny stitches at each mark along one edge.

Run a similar gathering thread up the other edge of ribbon, making sure that the stitches are exactly level on both sides. Gather up the loops as shown; it's easiest to knot the two threads together at one end of the gathers and ease the loops along.

Pull the thread tight to make properly-formed loops; sew the joins in place and cut off the excess thread. Tie the ribbon around the gift and use double-sided tape to attach the loops in the centre of the long side of the gift. Snip a diagonal cut at the ends of the ribbon tails.

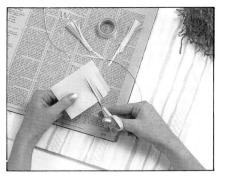

Disguise the unmistakable shape of a record by making it look like a cushion. First create paper tassels. Cut a piece of coloured paper into narrow strips leaving about 2.5cm (1in) at the bottom uncut so that you create a fringe. Roll up the fringe, catching in a short length of narrow ribbon. Secure the tassel with coloured tape.

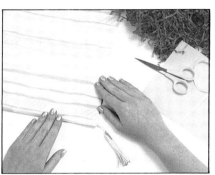

Take some wrapping paper that is more than twice the size of the gift, fold it in half around the record and cut it so that it is just a little larger. Join two of the sides together with coloured tape along their full length, attaching the ends of the tassels at the corners as you do so. Put a strip of tape over the folded edge of the 'bag'.

Stuff the inside of the 'bag' on both sides of the record with shredded tissue, being careful to put some in the corners. Don't use too much or the wrapping paper will wrinkle. Seal along the remaining open edge with tape.

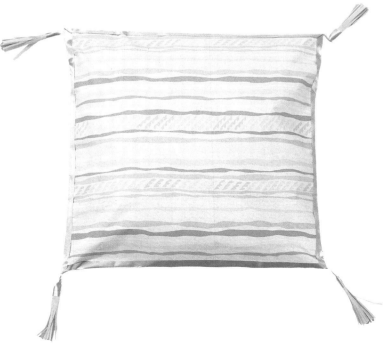

For an extra special gift at Christmas, wrap your present to look like a prayer book. Wrap the gift in gold paper so that it will look like the closed pages of the book. The last flap should not be folded in the usual way, but should be cut precisely to fit the side of the gift as shown; glue it in place.

Take two pieces of thick cardboard slightly larger than the size of the gift. You will also need a long strip of thin cardboard measuring the width and length of the gift. Use tape to stick the thick cardboard on to either side of the thin cardboard to make a book cover for the gift. Cover the outside with plain paper as shown; glue all the edges down firmly.

Spread glue over the inside of the book cover, and place the gift firmly on one side of it. Wrap the cover over the other side of the gift, making sure it's stuck properly. Cut out gold crosses (or other appropriate symbols relevant for your recipient's religion) and stick them in place.

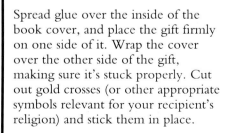

These sachets are ideal for ties, soaps, scarves, jewellery, hankies, socks and so forth. On to thin cardboard, trace the template on page 166. It's probably more interesting to cover the shape with gift wrap as shown here, but you can use plain cardboard if you wish. If using gift wrap, cut out the shape and paste it on to your chosen wrapping paper.

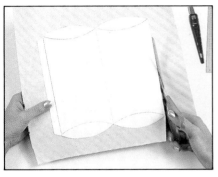

Cut out the covered shape. Then score well along the curved lines of the ellipses which will form the overlapping ends of the packet. Use the back of a craft knife or the blunt side of a pair of scissors to make the score marks.

Stick the side flaps together with either double-sided tape or glue. Fold in the ends; if you've scored the lines sufficiently they should pop in easily with just a little guidance. They can be re-opened with no difficulty, but make sure the covering gift wrap doesn't begin to lift off the cardboard.

A handy gift container, ideal for home-made sweets, can be made from a well-washed juice carton. Draw V-shapes in each side of the carton. These should be inverted on two opposite sides, and pointing towards the top of the carton on the other two sides. Cut cleanly along the drawn lines with a craft knife as shown.

Cover the carton with gift wrap; adhesive in spray form achieves the best results. Make sure the join lies neatly down one corner of the box. Trim the overlap at the top of the carton so that it is even and fold the paper over the edges, taking care that the corners are neat. Punch a hole at the apex of both the pointed sides and thread ribbon through.

This method is best suited to a small box as the end result is not particularly strong. From thin cardboard, cut out a cross-shaped piece as shown, made up of four sides and a base, all the same size and all absolutely square. The lid will also be a square measuring 5mm (¼in) larger than the base, with sides about 2cm (¾in) deep.

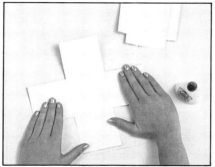

This small narrow box would be ideal for giving someone a watch or a piece of jewellery this Christmas. Trace off the template on page 95 on to thin cardboard. Cut it out, and either cover it in gift wrap or, if you like the colour of the cardboard, just leave it plain.

Cut around the template with small sharp scissors to trim away the excess gift wrap; take extra care with the slots and handles. Then score along all the fold lines, using the back of the craft knife or the blunt edge of the scissors.

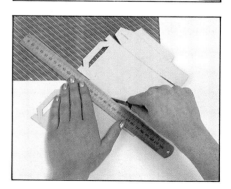

Paste both shapes on to gift wrap and when dry cut off the gift wrap around the box and lid, leaving a small turning or flap around each edge. Fold in the flap on the left of each side of the box and glue it down as shown. Score along the edges of what will be the base, to form fold lines for the sides of the box.

Bend the sides upwards. Put glue on the patterned side of the flaps of gift wrap left unfolded on each side; stick these flaps inside the box to the adjacent sides as illustrated. Crease down the sides firmly and leave to dry. Finally, fold in and glue the top lip. Treat the lid in exactly the same way.

Crease all the folds properly. Fold the box into shape and stick the side flap to the inside of the opposite side. Close the top section, being sure to fold the lid sections upright as shown, halfway across at the point where the two handles meet. Fold over the end flaps and slot them in position to close the box. Finally close the base.

TRIANGULAR TREAT

THE PYRAMIDS

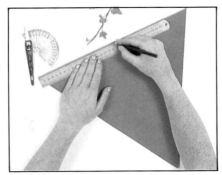

A plant is a notoriously difficult item to wrap; here's a smart solution. Measure an equilateral triangle on some coloured cardboard. The length of each side should be twice the height of the plant; use a protractor to ensure all the angles measure 60°

Divide each of the three sides of the triangle in half. Join all the half marks together to form an inner equilateral triangle; this will form the base. Bend the card along a ruler at each inner line as shown and bring up the sides to form a three-dimensional triangle. Punch a hole in each apex and thread ribbon through to close the parcel; double length ribbon gives a pretty finishing touch.

These rigid little boxes are ideal for presenting jewellery but you can make them to fit anything you like. Choose thin cardboard, either in the colour you want the finished box to be, or white so that you can cover it later with gift wrap. Measure out the template on page 166. The size of the triangular sides doesn't matter, as long as they are all the same, and the base is square.

Cut out along the exterior lines with a craft knife. If you're covering the cardboard shape with gift wrap, do it at this stage, cutting the paper to fit. Score along all the fold lines carefully, using the back of the craft knife, then bend the box along the score marks, creasing firmly.

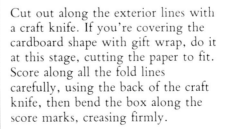
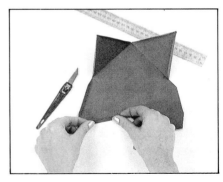

Punch holes in each apex and fold the box into its pyramidal shape. Thread the ribbon in and out of the four holes and, making sure all the side-folds are tucked inside the box, tie the loose ends together with a bow.

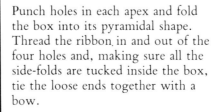

Smart handles give this box style; they are also the mechanism for closing it. Use coloured cardboard for the box; if you try to cover the box pattern with gift wrap it will lift off. Copy the template on page 166, scaling it up or down if you wish. Use a compass to draw the handles. Cut out the shape with a craft knife, taking great care with the handles and their slots.

Gift bags are very useful as containers for awkwardly-shaped presents and they can be made to any size. Find something with the required dimensions of the finished bag to serve as a mould — a pile of books should suffice. Choose a good quality, strong gift wrap for making the bag. Cut a strip of gift wrap long enough to wrap round the 'mould' and fold over the top edge.

Score along all the fold lines using the back of a craft knife; crease them well. Fold the carton into shape, and stick down the side flap with double-sided tape or glue. Fold the base down, pushing the flap inside the box to secure it.

Wrap the paper round the mould; glue or use double-sided tape to join the seam at the back. Fold over the end flaps in the usual way of wrapping any parcel to make the base of the bag; be sure to attach sufficient tape to make the base strong.

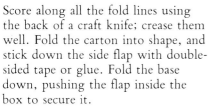

Close the first two flaps of the lid, folding the handles up to fit. Pinch the handles together and fold the two top flaps of the lid over them, fitting the handles through the slots.

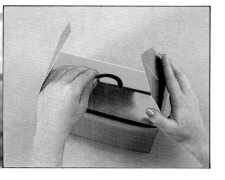

Slip the mould out. Fold in the sides of the bag, creasing them in half at the top; fold the base up over the back of the bag. Punch two holes, spaced apart, at the top of the front and back of the bag as shown. Thread through a length of cord to form a handle; knot each end inside the bag. Repeat on the other side. Alternatively, you could thread the bag with ribbon.

Making a box from scratch can be a little complicated, so why not start with an empty cereal packet? Take your cereal packet and carefully open it out flat. Separating the joins needs care – if necessary slide a knife between the seams to part the glue, rather than tear the packet.

This cube-shaped box is ideal for containing any kind of gift and it can be made to any size. Measure out the shape of the box on to thin cardboard, following the template on page 165. It's very important that all the squares are exactly the same size and that all the angles are right angles. Cut out the shape, and score along the fold lines – the back of a craft knife is useful for doing this.

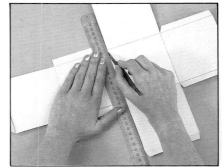

Draw the box you want, using the template on page 165 as a reference. Make sure the lid measures the same as the width of the side panels. Cut out the new shape with a pair of scissors, and cover it with your chosen gift wrap. Spray adhesive is best, since this gives a very smooth finish, however glue in a stick form will do. When the glue has dried, cut neatly around the cardboard shape.

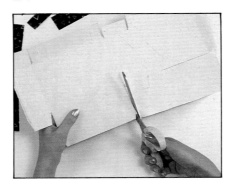

Bend the card carefully along the score lines, making a neat crease along each fold. Crease the flaps on the lid and base and fold the four sides into the shape of the box.

Score along the new fold lines of the box using the back of a craft knife or the blunt edge of a pair of scissors. Fold the box into shape. Stick the side flap in place as shown; you can use double-sided tape or glue. Fix the two flaps on the bottom (either glue them or tape them). Put in some shredded tissue as padding, slot in your gift and tuck the lid neatly in place.

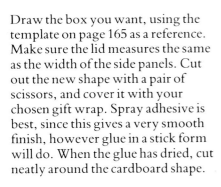

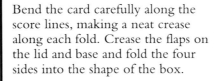

Stick the side flap to its opposite side as shown. You can glue this, or alternatively, use double-sided tape. Fold in the base flap – it should fit precisely and thus give the box rigidity. Finally, close the lid flap.

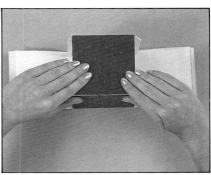

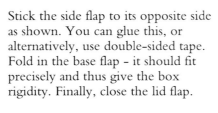

PUT A LID ON IT

IT'S A COVER-UP

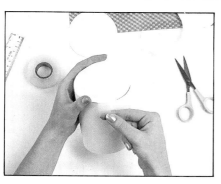

A cylindrical box looks much more difficult to make than it is. Wrap a piece of thin cardboard around the gift to determine the measurement of the box. Cut out the cardboard, roll it up and stick down the edge with a length of tape. Draw and cut out a circular base, and a slightly larger circle for the lid. Attach the base with small bits of tape.

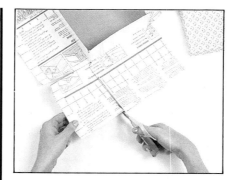

When re-covered in plastic, a shoe box makes a great container for a present. Put the box in the centre of a piece of self-adhesive plastic and draw around it. Then draw around the shape of the sides and ends of the box so you end up with a diagram of the 'exploded' box. Allow extra plastic all round for overlaps. Cut out the pattern you have just created.

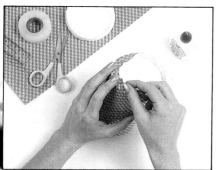

Cut a strip of cardboard slightly longer than the circumference of the cylinder. To make the lid, stick the edge of the strip to the edge of the circle with tape. Next, spread glue on some gift wrap and roll the cylinder in it. Cut the paper to fit, allowing an overlap each end. Tuck the overlap into the open end; secure. Fold the base overlap in a series of small triangles and stick to the base.

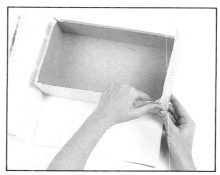

Peel the backing off the plastic and position the box carefully in the middle of the covering. Smooth the rest of the plastic up over the box, starting with the ends. Wrap the small overlap around the corners as shown.

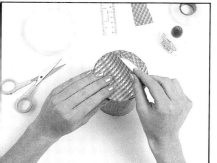

Draw a circle of gift wrap slightly smaller than the base. Cut it out and glue in position, hiding all the folds and bits of tape. Cover the lid in the same way. If you like, you can punch two holes in each side of the container and thread through short lengths of decorative braid.

Smooth the plastic up over the sides, trimming off the edges to make the pieces the exact size of the sides. Fold over the overlaps around the rim. Cover the lid in the same way. For complete co-ordination, you could cover the inside of the box to match. Alternatively, you could line the box with co-ordinating tissue paper or net.

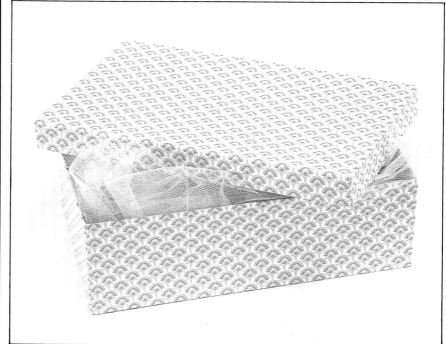

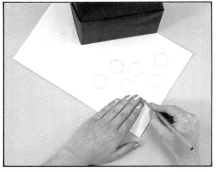

Cube-shaped presents will look more interesting disguised as dice — and it's fun if a small, flat gift becomes a domino. For the dice, make sure the gift is a perfect cube by measuring it; the idea won't work well unless it is. Cover the gift with black paper. Then draw several circles on white paper; an easy way of doing this is by tracing the outline of a suitably sized coin.

Cut out the circles carefully and lay them on the box; glue them in place. Look at a real dice to get the juxtaposition of the sides correct. The domino can be treated in the same way.

Brighten up a dull-looking, flat gift by turning it into a playing card. Wrap the present in plain white paper. Make a template for the spade by folding a piece of paper in half and drawing half the outline against the fold; this way the design will be symmetrical. Trace around the template on to black paper and cut the shape out. Stick the spade in the centre of the 'card'.

Cut two small spades for the corner designs. Then, using a ruler, draw an 'A' in two of the corners, being careful to make them both the same. Glue the small spades underneath. Cut a piece of patterned paper — smaller than the card — and stick it on the back.

Here's a clever idea for disguising a record. Get two large squares of cardboard; the side of a box will do. Position the record in one corner as shown and draw a line from the bottom right corner of the record to the top right corner of the cardboard. Draw a second rule from the top left corner of the record to complete the kite shape. Repeat for the other square.

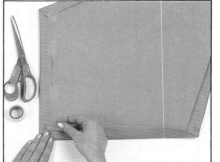

Cut out the shapes and sandwich the record between them. Cover one side in coloured paper, folding over the edges and fixing them with sticky tape on the reverse. Cut another piece of paper slightly smaller than the cardboard shape; glue it in position on the back of the kite.

Draw two lines joining the four corners of the kite, and put contrasting tape along them; take care not to stretch the tape as it will pucker the paper. Cut out as many paper bow shapes as you want for the kite's tail. Attach the bows with double-sided tape or glue to a length of ribbon and stick the tail in position behind the longest point of the kite.

Just the disguise for a cylinder-shaped gift this Xmas — the famous British red pillar-box (mailbox). Cut a strip of thin red cardboard to fit around your gift; secure it around the gift with sticky tape. Draw a circle for the lid, larger than the diameter of the cylinder; cut a line to its centre as shown.

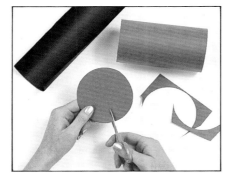

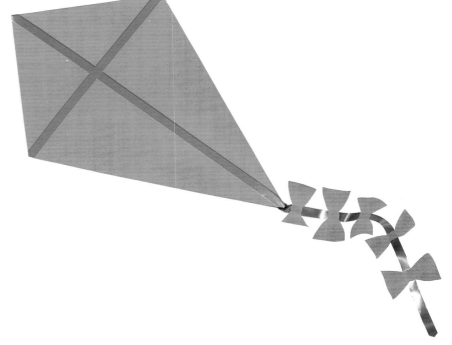

Overlap the cut edges slightly to form a shallow cone, then fix with sticky tape on the wrong side. Wrap one end of the post-box with black paper, folding it over to prevent the present from falling out. Put double-sided tape around the inside of the lid and stick in position. Add a narrow black rectangle for the posting slit and a white rectangle for the notice of collection times.

Disguise a bottle as a pencil and keep the recipient guessing! Make a cylinder, about 5cm (2in) shorter than the bottle, from light cardboard, join the sides with tape. Draw a third section of a circle— about 7.5cm (3in) radius—on pale cardboard and cut it out. Roll it in to a cone shape, running the flat edge of a pair of scissors along it to help it curl. Tape in place.

Make a small cone for the lead of the pencil and glue it on to the larger cone. Attach several lengths of sticky tape to the inside edge of the cone and, putting your arm inside the cylinder, stick the tape down to hold the cone in position. Fit the pencil over the bottle and secure with two strips of tape across the bottom.

Bottles of seasonal spirits make an ideal present — but hide such an obvious-looking gift under the decorative guise of a Christmas tree. Find a flower-pot just big enough to take the base of the bottle. From thin cardboard cut out a third section of a large circle and make a deep cone about 8cm (3in) shorter than the bottle. Cover the cone with suitable wrapping paper.

Put the bottle in the flower-pot and place the cone on top. You may need to trim the cone if it seems to cover too much of the flower-pot; do this with care, since you could easily make the cone too short! Double over a piece of tinsel, tie it in a knot and stick it on top of the 'tree'.

BUTTONS AND BOWS

FROSTY THE SNOWMAN

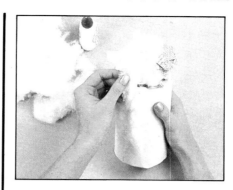

Make a small present look that extra bit special — and that extra bit bigger! Wrap the gift into a ball shape, then cut a strip of paper about three times the width of the gift and long enough to form loops on each side of it. Fold the edges over. Gather small pleats at each end, securing them with sticky tape. Pinch-pleat four gathers in the middle of the strip and secure.

What fun for a child to see Frosty and know that the snowman's hiding a gift! Wrap up a cylindrical gift in paper to form the body of the snowman. Crush newspaper into a shape for the head and stick it on top of the gift. Cover the body with cotton wool (absorbent cotton), sticking it on with dabs of glue. Create a face from bits of paper and stick in place.

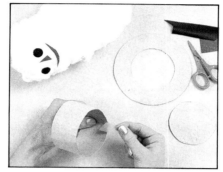

For the trailing sections of the bow, cut a five-sided piece of paper as shown. Fold over the edges in to the centre at the back and secure with tape. Gather pinch pleats at one end and secure. At the other end cut out a V-shaped section to form a nicely-shaped tail. Repeat the procedure a second time.

For the hat, you need a strip of cardboard, plus a circle big enough to make the brim. Draw an inner circle in the brim, the diameter of Frosty's head; cut it out to form the 'lid' of the hat. Roll the strip of cardboard up to form the crown of the hat; stick it in place with tape.

Turn the pleated ends of the long strip to the middle to form the loops, and secure with double-sided tape. Stick the tails under the bow with more tape. Finally, put double-sided tape over the join on top of the bow and stick the gift in position. Puff out the loops so they look nice and full.

Stick on the top of the hat, then attach the brim, putting strips of tape inside the crown. Paint the hat with black poster paint; it'll need two or three coats. Wrap around the red ribbon to form a cheery hat-band and put it on Frosty's head. Fray the ends of some patterned ribbon to form a scarf and tie it firmly in place.

Wit so many presents being exchanged at this time of the year, tags are very important. And they are so easy to make. Draw any festive shape you like on to thin cardboard; this one is a Christmas stocking. Cut out the shape and cover it with bright paper; try to co-ordinate the colours with those in the gift wrap you use for your present.

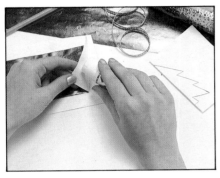

If your wrapping paper has a particular theme in its design make a tag to echo it. To ensure that your design is symmetrical, fold a piece of paper in half and draw on half the design against the fold. Cut around the outline through both layers of paper; open out and use this as a template for the design. Cover a piece of light cardboard with gift wrap and trace around the template.

Cut around the outline and punch a hole at the top of the tag. Write your message and tie the tag on to the parcel. You could cheat a little when designing the shape of your tag by tracing an illustration from a magazine or by using the outline of a pastry cutter.

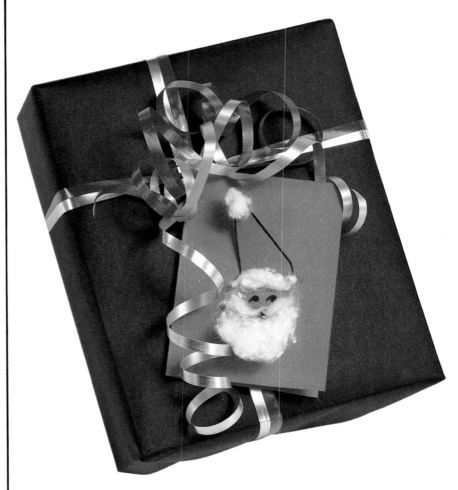

A three-dimensional Santa Claus tag, complete with fluffy beard, provides a jolly festive decoration on a gift. Draw a fairly large rectangle on thin red cardboard; make sure that all the corners are right angles. Score down the middle and fold the cardboard, creasing it well. Draw an inverted 'V' for Santa's hat, and a curve for his chin; cut them out with a craft knife.

Curve the hat and chin outward to give them a three-dimensional look, then draw in the eyes and mouth. Form a beard from a small piece of cotton wool (absorbent cotton), and stick it in position with a dab of glue. Do the same with the fur trim on the edge of the hat and the pom-pom on its tip. Punch a hole in the back of the label, write your message and tie the tag on the parcel.

A heavenly messenger bears the greetings on this Christmas present. Cut a quarter section of a circle from light cardboard to form a narrow cone for the body. On a folded piece of paper draw one arm and one wing against the edge of the fold as shown, so that when they are cut out you will have a pair of each.

Make the cone and cover it with silver paper (aluminium foil would do). Trace the arm and wings on to silver paper; cut them out and glue them in their relevant positions on the body.

Used greeting cards can often be turned into very acceptable gift tags. Sometimes, as here, the design lends itself to forming a tag. Cut very carefully around the lines of the motif you want to use. Make a hole with a punch, thread a ribbon through the hole and no one would guess the tag had a previous life!

Sometimes a little imagination is needed to give the tag a new and ready-made look. Here, the shape of the tag is outlined on the cardboard in red with a felt-tipped pen. Draw the outline lightly in pencil first to be absolutely sure it is the right size and shape to create the finished label.

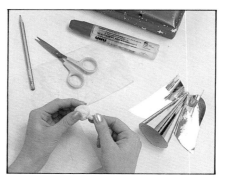

Make the head by rolling up some white tissue paper into a firm ball, twisting the ends of the tissue tightly to form a 'neck'. Glue the head into the top of the cone. Tie a scrap of tinsel into a loose knot and stick it on the head as a halo. Make a scroll from white paper, write on your message and stick it between the angel's hands. Attach the angel to the gift with double-side tape.

FUN FOLD-OUT

GIFT BOX TAGS

I f you have a long message for the recipient of your gift, this fold-out tag allows lots of room. Select a gift wrap design that has a fairly large repeat. One motif must have sufficient space around it so that it can be cut out without including any others. Draw a rectangle around the motif, ensuring that all the corners are right angles.

Cut the rectangle out with a craft knife. Next, cut out a piece of thin cardboard the same height as the chosen motif and exactly three times its width. Fold the cardboard in three widthways, creasing the folds well, then fold the top two sections back on themselves, as shown. Mark the folds in pencil first to be sure they are straight.

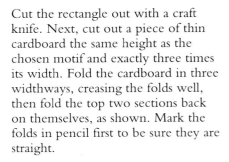

Cut the motif from the gift wrap precisely in half. Glue each half on to the top two sections of the folded card. They should fit exactly, but if necessary trim the top and bottom to form a straight edge. Try matching the colours of the lining cardboard with the gift wrap; in the example shown here, red or even black could have been used, instead of white, for a different effect.

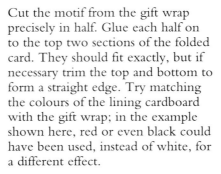

T hese effective tags are a useful way of using up scraps of cardboard left over from larger projects. Cut a card 10cm x 5cm (4in x 2in), score and fold in half. Measure 6mm ($^1/_4$in) down from the fold and mark 2mm ($^1/_8$in) in from the sides before cutting through both thicknesses with a craft knife to give a 'lid' shape. Run the blade along the steel ruler twice for a clean edge.

Punch a hole through both thicknesses at the centre top. Glue on ribbons in a cross shape, folding the raw edges over to the inside of the tag. Finish off with a bow or curled gift wrap ribbon tied through the hole at the top. The tags can be made up in any size or colour with contrasting ribbons to match your gift.

STARS AND STRIPES

IT'S A STICK UP

M atch the label to the paper by creating a larger version of a shape which appears in the gift wrap. Begin by drawing a scaled-up shape of the motif from the paper and use it as a template from which to trace the design onto coloured cardboard.

For this idea to be really effective, the colour of the tag should be as close as possible to that in the gift wrap. A layer of tissue laid over cardboard of a near-match, as shown, might make all the difference to duplicating the final colour. Cut out the shape, and punch a hole to enable you to tie it to the gift.

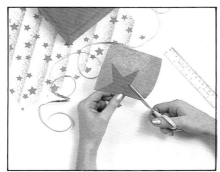

T here is such a variety of stickers on the market that you're sure to find one which will make an ideal label for your gift. Take a piece of thin coloured cardboard; this will form the background for the sticker. Draw a rectangle on to the cardboard, twice the width you wish the finished tag to be.

Cut out the rectangle with a craft knife and score down the centre to form the fold; crease well. Remove the sticker from its backing and place it in position on the front of the tag. Punch a hole in the back 'page' of the tag near the fold. Write your message inside and hang the tag on the gift.

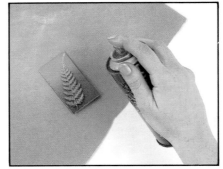

Press some flowers and foliage to make these pretty gift tags. Cut a piece each of red metallic and glossy white cardboard 7.5cm x 10cm (3in x 4in) and fold widthways. Secure a tip of fern to the front of the red card. Spray with gold paint and when dry, lift off the fern, leaving a red silhouette. Fix the gold fern to the front of the white card. Punch a hole and thread with ribbon.

Cut a piece of single-sided glossy green cardboard 7.5cm x 10cm (3in x 4in). Crease and fold 4cm (1½in) from the left edge to give a folded card size of 7.5cm x 6cm (3in x 2½in). With a green marker pen, draw a border inside the larger page. Fix a spray of miniature rose leaves in one corner then form a loose line of guelder rose flowers up the page.

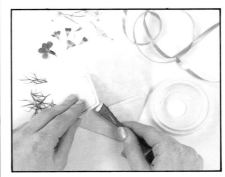

Having looked at the construction of an envelope make a miniature version from a 14cm (5½in) square of paper. Glue the envelope together and line the side flaps with a silver marker. Take wispy foliage, gypsophila and mauve lobelia and secure them inside the envelope so that they appear to be bursting out. Attach some curled mauve ribbon to the top of the tag.

Take some red and green single-sided cardboard and cut out some sock shapes. Using gold or silver aerosol paint, spray heads of fools' parsley; when dry, secure the best shaped florets to the heels and toes of the socks. Draw a ribbed border at the top of each sock, punch a small hole in the corner, and add coloured ties.

Crease and fold a small piece of yellow cardboard in half and, with your compass pencil just overlapping the fold, draw a 6.5cm (2½in) circle. Cut this out, leaving the card hinged together by about 3cm (1¼in) at the top. Draw a 5cm (2in) circle in green marker pen on the front cover and fix three daisies in the middle. Refold the card and fix a length of thin green ribbon about the fold.

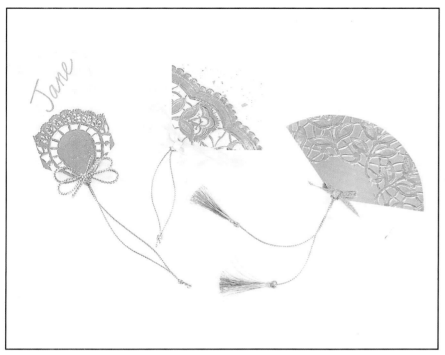

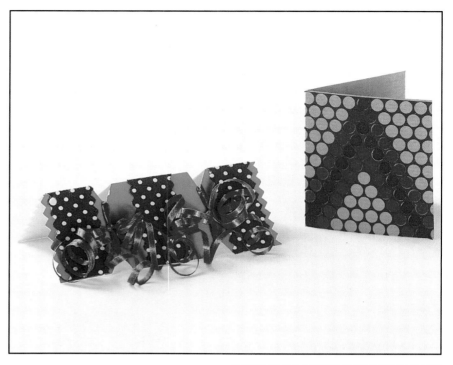

Cut out tags in coloured cardboard or speckled paper. Either cut a single tag and write the message on the back or fold the card in half and cut out a double tag where the message will be inside. Cut a section from a gold paper doily and stick it to the front with spray glue. Trim away any excess level with the edges of the tag.

To make this dotty Christmas tag, make a cracker-shaped template and trace around it onto brightly coloured cardboard. Reverse the template along one long edge and trace around it again. Cut out the tag and fold it in half. Use pinking shears to trim the ends. Cut three strips of florists' ribbon to fit across the cracker. Pink the edges and spray glue them to the cracker.

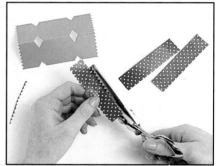

Pierce a hole on a corner of the tag with the points of a pair of scissors. Cut a length of fine gold cord and bend it in half. Insert the ends through the hole and pull through the loop. Knot the cord ends together or sew them to small gold tassels for extra style.

Tie two pieces of giftwrap ribbon around 'ends' of the cracker as shown. Split the ribbon down the centre and curl each length against a scissor blade.

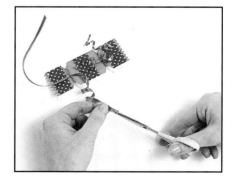

To decorate the tags further you can write the recipient's name in gold pen and glue on a bow.

Cut a card 15cm x 7.5cm (6in x 3in), score and fold in half. Cut a piece of sequin waste to fit and attach to the front of the card with spray glue. Colour in circles with felt-tipped pens, many different patterns can be made. Punch a hole in back and thread with ribbon.

Cut a gold card 30cm x 15cm (12in x 6in) and score 7.5cm (3in) in from each side. Trace off the template on page 165 and carefully work out where the points will fall. Mark the design on the back of the gold card and cut out using a sharp craft knife and ruler for straight edges.

Cut the kings' gifts from gold card and glue in place. Attach sequins to the points of their crowns. Stick on a piece of white card to cover the back of the centre panel. To protect the points, slip a further piece of card into the envelope. The three kings which have been cut out could be used for a further card or gift tag.

Burnish the edges of the gold card with the back of your thumb nail if they have lifted. Cut king's clothes from three pieces of brocade, slightly larger than the apertures. Place small pieces of double-sided tape around the kings on the inside of the card and stick brocade in place.

N ew Year celebrations are particularly associated with Scotland. So here, in traditional Scottish style, we have tartan and golden bells for our New Year greeting. A ready-cut window card was used. Remove the left-hand section off a 3-fold card with a sharp craft knife and ruler. Use this spare card to make two bells.

C ut a card 15cm x 22cm (6in x 8½in), score and fold in half widthways. Mark the centre top of the card with a pencil dot. Cut a triangle from sequin waste and stick centrally on the card applying a little glue around the edges only. Hold in place on the card until the glue dries. Any residue glue can be rubbed away afterwards.

Cut a piece of tartan fabric or paper to fit inside the back of the card, attach with spray glue and trim the edges. Draw two bell shapes onto the spare gold card. Cut out and back with tartan using spray glue. Trim with small scissors and punch holes in the top.

Cut a base for the tree from a piece of cardboard or paper. Curl over scissors a number of pieces of narrow gift wrap ribbon, cut about 9.5cm (3¾in) long.

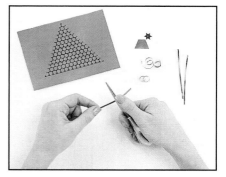

Make a bow from narrow satin ribbon and cut a length of ribbon for the bells to hang from. Thread the first bell and hold in place with a dab of glue, then thread the second bell. Sew the bow onto the card, above the aperture, and through the ribbon suspending the bells.

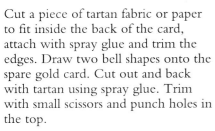

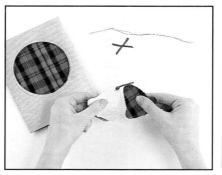

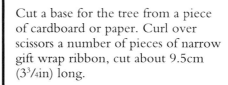

Glue on the base and add a sequin star to the top of the tree. Slip the curled ribbons through every other hole in the sequin waste and every other row, starting at the top of the tree. You shouldn't have to glue them as they will stay in place. But you will need to deliver this card by hand if it is not to get squashed.

Cut a green card 15cm x 20cm (6in x 8in) and score down the centre. Draw one half of a Christmas tree and cut out a paper template. Draw around this onto the green card, reversing the template along the scored line; cut out. Set your sewing machine to a wide satin stitch and, moving the card from side to side, sew the garlands. Pull loose threads through to the back and knot.

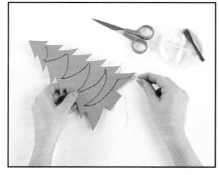

Decorate the tree with self-adhesive spots to resemble Christmas tree baubles. Then cut narrow satin ribbon into fourteen 1cm (1/2in) strips.

Glue strips in place at the end of the branches on the back of the card: tweezers will help you to hold them steady. Leave until the glue dries, then cut the tops diagonally to look like candles. Add the finishing touch with a red star on top of the tree.

On red fabric, draw four 9cm (31/2in) squares and cut them out. Fold in a 6mm (1/4in) seam allowances and press. Find the centre of each square by folding it diagonally twice and press with the tip of an iron. Open out the squares, then fold the corners into the centre. Catch the centre points with a small stitch. Fold in again and sew along the seams!

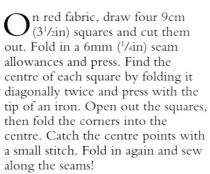

Cut four 2cm (3/4in) squares from fir-tree fabric. Place two red squares right sides together and sew down one side to make a double square. Pin a fir-tree patch diagonally over the seam on the right side, and curl back the red folds surrounding the patch to cover the raw edges. Slip stitch to hold in place. Repeat to make another double square.

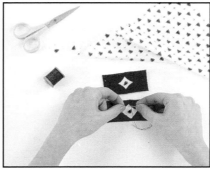

Sew the double squares together and place a third and fourth fir-tree patch over the seams. Sew tiny beads in the corners. Cut a card 25cm x 18cm (10in x 7in), score and fold in half. Mark the top centre and 6cm (21/2in) down either side. Cut out to form a point. Glue the finished square onto the card and draw a border with a gold felt-tip pen.

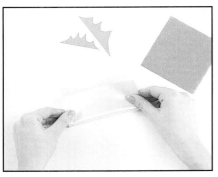

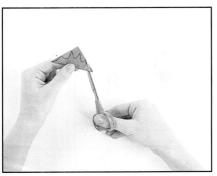

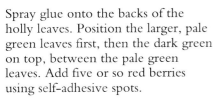

Cut a silver card 30cm x 15cm (12in x 6in), score and fold in half widthways. Trace the holly templates from page 165 and transfer onto thin cardboard. Cut a 13cm (5in) square of green satin paper and a 10cm (4in) square of dark green tissue paper. Fold both squares in half twice, then diagonally to make a triangle.

Cut out the larger holly from satin paper and unfold, then the smaller holly in dark green paper. Hold the holly templates in place on the paper triangles with paper clips when cutting out. Or you can draw around the templates first if you find it easier.

Spray glue onto the backs of the holly leaves. Position the larger, pale green leaves first, then the dark green on top, between the pale green leaves. Add five or so red berries using self-adhesive spots.

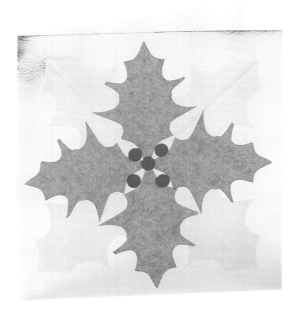

Add a musical note to your greetings this Christmas. The treble clefs are buttons. Cut a glossy red card 22cm x 15cm (8½in x 6in). Score and fold in half widthways. Draw a square 5.5cm x 7.5cm (2¼in x 3in) on white paper. Rule two staves – groups of five lines 3mm (⅛in) apart – using a fine black felt-tipped pen. Cut out the square.

Centre the square of music paper on the card so that you have an equal margin on three sides. Visually, it is better to have a larger margin at the base of the card. Mark the corners of the music sheet lightly on the card and stick down using spray glue. Place the opened card on a piece of felt and pierce two holes for the two buttons using dividers or a thick needle.

From the back, sew on the buttons through the holes you have pierced, then knot the thread and trim. Finish the knots with a dab of glue.

To make these quick festive cards, we purchased some ready-cut 3 fold cards, and used stickers and buttons to decorate them. Cut three strips of fabric in suitable colours: here blue glitter-spotted material has been used for the sky, silver lamé for the frozen landscape and white towelling for the snow.

Cut out the sections and sew buttons in place or attach stickers. Using double-sided tape, mount the pieces over the back of the apertures and glue the extra flap down on each card. Extra sequins can be added to the borders for the moon or stars.

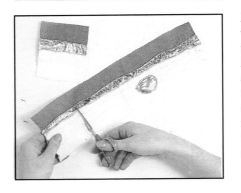

Machine the strips together with a wide satin stitch, machining over twice if you want a thicker line. Measure the size of the card's aperture and mark cutting lines on the fabric. Machine trees with lines of stitches, or cut circles of lamé and make ponds. Use your imagination to dream up a different idea for each card.

A dove of peace for New Year. It is made from a paper doiley with calendar dates falling from its beak. Cut a deep blue card 30cm x 20cm (12in x 8in), score and fold in half. Draw freehand two curves at the top of the front of the card to represent clouds and cut with a craft knife.

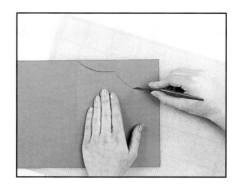

Trace the dove pattern from page 165 and transfer to thin cardboard to make your own template. Trace out a dove onto a white paper doiley and cut out, together with the dates 1 and 31 from an old calendar. Also cut a strip of translucent film, making it wavy along the upper edge to resemble hills.

Make a template from the pattern on page 165 and cut an extra template for the wing (see finished card). Draw round the dove twice on dark blue felt so that the birds face opposite directions. Cut them out. Cut two pieces of muslin 18cm x 11.5cm (7in x 4½in), position the doves between both layers and pin. Tack the layers together to hold the doves in place.

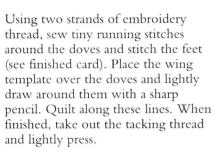

Using two strands of embroidery thread, sew tiny running stitches around the doves and stitch the feet (see finished card). Place the wing template over the doves and lightly draw around them with a sharp pencil. Quilt along these lines. When finished, take out the tacking thread and lightly press.

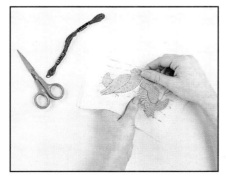

Spray glue all the pieces and place on the card together with four star sequins. Finally, using a felt-tipped silver pen, draw a line along the edge of the cloud curves.

Purchase a 3-fold window card to fit the quilted doves. Cut out a matching window from the left-hand section of the card. Trim the muslin to about 6mm (¼in) larger than the window. Stick the quilt down using double-sided tape. Add tiny round beads for the doves' eyes and pearl beads to the corners of the window.

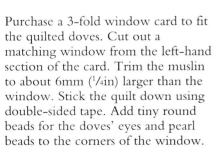

Make a traditional Christmas card from pressed ferns. Cut a rectangle of white cardboard 16.5cm x 6.5cm (6¹⁄₂in x 2¹⁄₂in). Select a piece of bracken about 14cm (5¹⁄₂in) in length. Fix the bracken to the card with spots of glue. Leave sufficient space at the base of this 'tree' for the 'flower pot'. For the star, spray a floret of fools' parsley gold, and glue to the top of the tree.

From red metallic board cut a rectangle 21.5cm x 20cm (8¹⁄₂in x 8in); crease, and fold in half lengthways. Now draw a rectangle – larger than the white card using a gold marker. Cut out a 'flower pot' from some red board, draw on some decorative lines and fix the pot to the tree. Cover the design card with protective film and fix it centrally within the gold border.

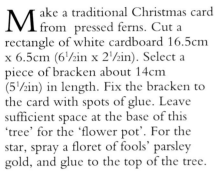

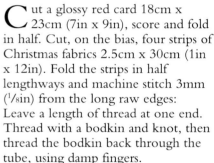

Cut a glossy red card 18cm x 23cm (7in x 9in), score and fold in half. Cut, on the bias, four strips of Christmas fabrics 2.5cm x 30cm (1in x 12in). Fold the strips in half lengthways and machine stitch 3mm (¹⁄₈in) from the long raw edges: Leave a length of thread at one end. Thread with a bodkin and knot, then thread the bodkin back through the tube, using damp fingers.

Thread a length of double wool through each tube. Pin the ends of the tubes to a firm surface. To plait them, lay all four strands over the left hand, then take the left strand over the two middle strands and the right strand over one. Continue in this way to the end. Ease into a circle, cross over the ends and sew through to secure. Trim and finish with a bow.

Bind the trimmed ends with embroidery cotton. Draw an arched border onto the card using a gold pen. Centre the finished wreath and pierce through the card with a thick needle. Sew through from the back of the card to hold the garland in place. Knot the thread, trim and finish with a dot of glue to hold firm.

A simple, easily-made card in unusual colours for Christmas. Cut a card 11cm x 20cm (4¼in x 8in), score and fold in half. Keep the fold at the top of the card. Cut a strip of green plastic from an old shopping bag. Tear four strips of tissue in shades of orange and yellow. The fir-tree is taken from a strip of self-adhesive stickers.

Arrange the strips so that the colours overlap and produce new colours and tones. Stick the tree in place, then spray glue onto the backs of the strips and stick down also.

A friendly snowman invites you to come outside to play. Cut off the left-hand side of a 3-fold card so that light will shine through the window. Cut a piece of film slightly smaller than the folded card. Draw a snowman and trees on to paper to fit between the window bars. Place the paper under the film and trace the outline of the snowman and trees with a silver pen.

Turn the film over and colour in the trees and the snowman using a white chinagraph pencil.

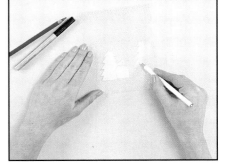

Trim any excess paper from the edges of the card with a sharp craft knife and steel ruler.

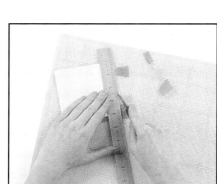

Turn the film the right way up and draw a scarf and nose with a red chinagraph pencil. Add face details in silver. Attach the film to the inside of the card with double-sided tape and place a silver star where it can be seen shining through the window.

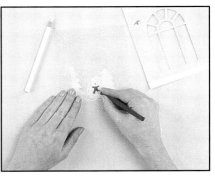

There is a surprise for the person who opens this card. Cut a rectangle of blue cardboard 20cm x 16cm (8in x 6¼in). Score widthwise across the centre and fold in half. Tear white paper into strips and glue across the lower edge on the front and inside. Cut out two green trees from thin cardboard and glue to the front.

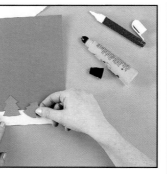

Paint snowflakes with a white typing correction pen. Use the template on page 164 to cut out the snowman in white cardboard, the hat and scarf in yellow and the eyes, nose and buttons in black. Draw a pattern on the scarf and hat with a red pen. Glue all the pieces to the snowman and draw a smile with a black felt-tipped pen.

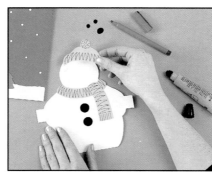

Score along the centre of the snowman and the broken lines on the tabs. Bend the snowman in half along the scored centre and place him inside the card matching the fold to the opening edges of the card and keeping the lower edges level. Glue the tabs inside the card.

Cut a card 18cm x 23cm (7in x 9in). Score and fold in half. Draw a border in silver pen around the card. Make a sock-shaped template out of thin cardboard and draw around it onto red felt using a water-soluble pen. Now hold the template in place over some sequin waste and cut around it.

Sew the sequin waste to the felt by hand or machine, then trim both layers neatly.

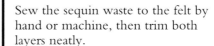

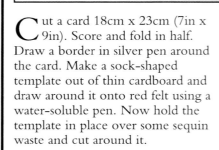

Glue the stocking to the card, then add the little pony eraser or another small gift that can be glued on. Draw holly and berries using felt-tipped pens. You could also add beads and sequins if you wish.

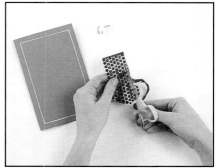

Colourful puffins, cut from a sheet of wrapping paper, keep a lookout from their perch. Cut a card 28cm x 13cm (18in x 5¼in). The card should be blue on the inside and white on the outside. On the outside, score lines 9cm (3½in) and 19cm (7½in) in from the left and fold. Turn the card over and on the inside score and fold 20cm (8in) in from the left.

Cut out three puffins and spray glue the first one on to the outside of the far right-hand panel of card, facing right. Cut around him with a craft knife leaving him attached to the card by his tail. The score line on the outside will allow him to stand forward.

Glue the other two puffins in place on the inside. Any wrapping paper with a distinct animal motif can be used in this way to make a striking card.

Cut a card 23cm x 18cm (9in x 7in), score and fold in half. Trace the pattern from page 165 and transfer it onto thin cardboard to make a template. Place on some polystyrene wallpaper and draw around it with a soft pencil. Cut out with a craft knife. Also cut out some ice caps and ground from iridescent plastic or silver paper.

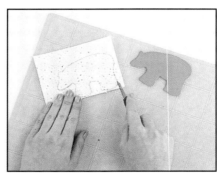

Glue down the mountains, ground and polar bear, placing the latter in front of the peaks. Then decorate with silver sequin stars.

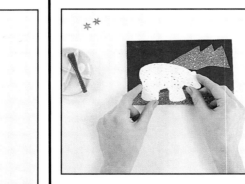

With a silver pen draw in the polar bear's features: the legs, paws and ears. As an alternative, the polar bear could also be made from white felt.

In this section, we demonstrate that a hand-made gift can look both stylish and professional, and be a delight to the recipient. Floral gifts are ideal for female friends and relatives; we have selected a range of ideas to choose from, from pot-pourri bags and picture frames to attractive floral arrangements. For the men in your life, there are desk sets, stationery, photograph frames and modern decorative ornaments, such as the ducks on page 152. We've also included soft toys for the children – or your big sister! – and a number of items which you can enhance by painting: plates, pots and china as well as tea cosies and potato print cushions.

These tiny pot-pourri bags are so easy to create, and they make delightful gifts. Take a length of cotton fabric and, using a plate as a pattern, cut out a circle about 25-30cm (10-12in) in diameter. Hem the edge with running stitch, leaving long tails of thread at either end. Cup the fabric circle in your hand as shown and fill it with pot-pourri.

Gather the fabric into a tight ball by pulling the threads. Secure with a knot. Wire together a small tight bunch of helichrysum (strawflower or everlasting) using fine silver rose wire and attach the posy to the bag, threading the wire through the fabric on both sides to secure. (Use a needle to make holes in the fabric first if necessary.)

Make a double bow out of satin ribbon and wire this on to the bag. finally, cut a length of gold cord about 35cm (15in) long and tie it round the posy, finishing with a double knot. Tie the ends of the cords at the desired length and hang the bag by this loop.

Combine an antique pot with dried flowers for the perfect gift. Note how the blue and orange in the china have been picked up by the colours of the flowers. First, cut a block of florists' foam to fit snugly inside the pot.

Using wired bunches of helichrysum (strawflower or everlasting), build up a dome shape to reflect the shape of the pot. Then add clusters of blue-dyed *Leucodendron brunia*. The unusual bobbly shape of this plant will always add interest to any arrangement.

Finally, add clumps of bright yellow morrison to fill in any gaps and complete the display.

In this attractive design, dried flowers have been used to form a picture. Take a small oval frame and remove the glass, leaving only the backing board. Cut the heads off a colourful selection of plants and start to glue them on to the board. Begin with a red rose in the middle, surrounded by bright yellow yarrow. Add red celosia cockscomb next.

Continue to arrange the heads in small groups, covering the entire surface. The other plants used here are love-in-a-mist heads inside bells of Ireland, lotus seedheads and silver bobbles of *Leucodendron brunia*. The picture is completed with some pearl achillea (a type of yarrow) dotted in amongst the *Leucodendron*.

ALL AROUND MY HAT

A small straw hat, decorated with a garland of dried flowers, makes a pretty gift. This particular hat is a small doll's hat. Begin by making three double bows out of satin ribbon. Tie a second length of ribbon round the middle of one of the bows to form the long 'tails' at the back of the hat.

Make a garland to wrap around the crown as follows. Attach some rose wire to a length of string, about 20-25cm (8-10in) from one end. Place a small bunch of flowers over the join and secure with the wire. Add another bunch to cover the stems of the first and bind as before. Continue adding to the garland in this way until it is the desired length.

The flowers used in this garland are red amaranthus (love-lies-bleeding), south African daisy (helichrysum) and golden dyandra. Wrap the garland round the crown and tie the ends of the string together to secure. Wire a couple of bows to the front of the hat and put the other one over the join at the back.

NEPTUNE'S GOLD

Three clam shells provide the perfect setting for a colourful miniature arrangement. First you must carefully bore a hole in the base of each shell using a braddle. Now fix the shells together with wire, fanning two of them out as shown and using the third as a base. Slice a section off a sphere of florists' foam and cut it to fit the base of the shells. Glue the foam in position.

Cut off a number of honesty (silver dollar plant) seedheads and insert them singly into the foam, covering it completely. Next add small wired bunches of tiny red roses, concentrating them in the middle. Follow with clumps of golden quaking grass, positioning them so that they fan out from the centre of the arrangement and form a star-shaped outline.

Fill in amongst the quaking grass with clumps of bright yellow cluster-flowered helichrysum (strawflower or everlasting), packing them tightly into the arrangement.

BRASS SHELL

LATE SUMMER ROSES

In this attractive arrangement, peachy coloured dried flowers set off a small brass trinket box to perfection. Cut a section from a cylinder of florists' foam to fit inside the box and secure with a strip of florists' tape.

Build up the shape of the display with cluster-flowered sunray and a few strands of creamy nipplewort (or broom bloom). The latter will add a fluffy softness to the arrangement.

Next add the focal flowers which are peachy South African daisies (a type of helichrysum). Wire them in small groups and intersperse them throughout. Finish off with a few cones to add an interesting contrast of colour and texture.

A jet black wooden box provides a frame for this pretty dried flower arrangement, and helps to bring out the subtle warmth of the roses. Cut a block of florists' foam to fit the box and wedge it tightly in place. If the fit is good there should be no need to tape it.

Build up the outline using wired bunches of white bupleurum. Keep the shape well within that of the box. Start to fill in the outline with South African daisies (a type of helichrysum), using them to cover the foam. Make the flowers shorter at the front of the display, slightly overhanging the edge of the box.

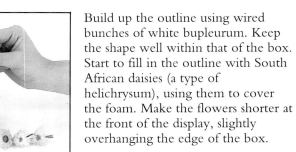

Complete the picture with several rust-coloured roses, recessing some deep into the arrangement. Gently pull back the outer petals if necessary to open out the flowers before you position them.

This imaginative gift is ideal for displaying in a kitchen. Cut a sphere of florists' foam in two and tape one half on the side of an old flour sieve. Build up a spiky outline using ears of wheat, pushing them singly into the foam. Keep the arrangement asymmetrical by making the stems longer on one side so that they spill out of the bottom of the 'frame'.

Follow the general outline already created using pink larkspur, keeping it as tall as the wheat. Intersperse the arrangement with South African daisies (a type of helichrysum). Place them at varying heights, then add depth with several bunches of moon grass, pushing them well into the display.

Complete the picture with a small posy on top of the sieve; wire together a small group of plants, then cover the wire with raffia. Finish off with a bow and glue the posy on to the sieve.

A host of tiny dried flowers and grasses cluster round an old but gleaming brass bell, creating a very pretty effect. Cut a slice from a cylinder of florists' foam then cut the slice in half. Gouge out the centre of the two halves and affix the pieces to the handle as shown, using tape.

Build up the shape of the arrangement using single stems of mauve xeranthemum. Position those at the top of the display upright, and those lower down dangling over the bell. Now intersperse with wired clumps of quaking grass, following the same outline. Finish off with bunches of lady's mantle, pushed well into the arrangement.

CAUSE A STIR

DAYS IN THE DAIRY

A couple of old wooden spoons form the basis of a pretty arrangement that would brighten up any kitchen. First, wire the spoons together at an angle as shown, winding the wire round the handles several times to secure firmly.

Wire together several small groups of plants, choosing an attractive range of colours. Shown here is yellow quaking grass, white helichrysum (strawflower or everlasting) and dudinea seedheads. Wire the small groups together to form one large bunch and attach this to the spoons so that the blooms sit prettily over the bowls.

Make a large bright double bow out of satin ribbon and tie it with a second length of ribbon around the spoons and the posy.

A pair of butter pats makes an unusual setting for this kitchen design. Take a length of ribbon and wire up one end. Thread the ribbon through both holes from the front, leaving a long tail between the pats. Loop the ribbon over the top and thread through from the front again, pulling it tight. Make a second loop in the same way, leaving it long for hanging the display.

Secure the wired end of ribbon at the back with a knot; cut off any excess. Wire a small bow on to the front of the pats. Then attach half a sphere of florists' foam to the ribbon 'tail' using tape. Wire small bunches of blue jasilda and tiny red helichrysum and push them into the ball, packing them tightly together.

Add longer stems of blue larkspur, leaving some pieces trailing down the pats to break up the outline of the ball. Finally, wire up short double loops of ribbon and intersperse them among the flowers, finishing off with a couple of longer strands at the bottom.

Pressed flower specimens hung on a ruby satin bow make the perfect gift. Take 2½m (2¾yd) of 7.5cm (3in) wide ribbon, and cut it into three lengths: 50cm (20in), 58cm (23in), and 1.42m (56in). Fold the shortest length, ends to centre, to form a bow and gather the centre using needle and thread. Do the same with the next longest length.

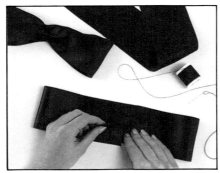

Place the smaller bow on top of the larger one, gather them tightly at the centre, and stitch together. Fold the longest length approximately in half around the centre of the double bow, and sew together at the back to form the knot of the finished bow. Also sew in a small curtain ring at the back by which to hang the design. Trim the ends of the ribbon as shown.

Cut three ovals from beige cartridge paper to fit some miniature plaques. Using a fine pen, write the botanical names of your specimens neatly at the bottom of the ovals. For the first oval, arrange stems, foliage and flowers of forget-me-not to simulate a growing plant. When satisfied with their positioning, fix down with latex adhesive and re-assemble the plaque.

For the second oval, take a large heart's ease and fix it one third of the way up from the base, then add further flowers finishing with the smallest at the top. Now introduce heart's ease leaves to give the appearance of a vigorous young plant. When satisfied, fix in position and then carefully assemble within the plaque.

Place a curved stem in the centre of the third oval and fix borage flowers and buds along the stem in a natural way so that it resembles the top of a growing stem. As before, when you have completed the picture, assemble the plaque. Take the three plaques, and arrange them down the ribbon at regular intervals. Now sew them in place, parting the ribbons slightly.

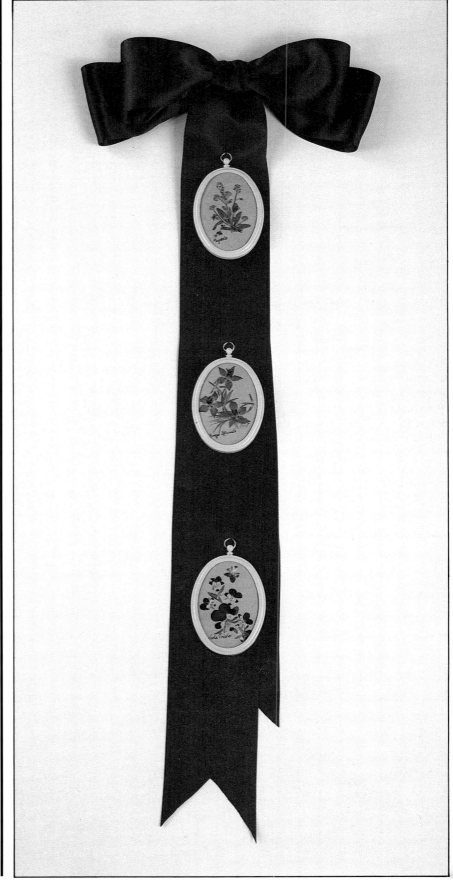

C apture the beauty of a rose in this charming pressed flower design. You will need a round frame 15cm (6cm) in diameter. Cut a mount from coloured paper, then cut a white card to fit the frame. Lay the mount over the white card and lightly pencil in the aperture. Fix single rose leaves in a ring, overlapping, with the tips about 3mm (¹/8in) from the pencilled circle.

Select large rose petals and repeat the process, with the top of the petals overlapping the leaves by 6mm (¹/4in). Both the leaves and petals need to be fixed with very small dabs of latex adhesive. When the glue has dried, carefully rub out the pencil line and blow away the rubbings.

T hese glass drinks coasters - easily available from craft shops - lend themselves to a pressed carnation display and will make a most welcome gift. Cut a circle of moss green cartridge paper to fit into the recess of the large bottle coaster. Now fix large petals of yellow carnation, overlapping them slightly, to form an outer circle.

Fill in the outer circle with smaller carnation petals to create a second circle. Small petals from the centre of the carnation make up the final inner circle. To complete the display fix cow parsley florets to the centre.

Now form an inner circle with smaller petals in the same way. Select the centre part of a rock rose, put a small dot of adhesive right in the middle of the rose ring and, using a palette knife, slide the rock rose into position. Finally, place the mount over the design card, being careful to centre it, and position the cleaned glass over both. Transfer them to the frame and secure the back.

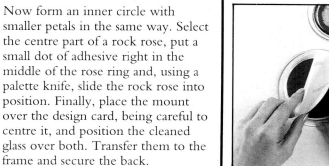

Fit the design card into the recess of the bottle coaster and seal with the circle of baize supplied. Repeat this process for each drinks coaster, using different colours for an attractive display.

A striking tray, purchased from craft suppliers, makes a perfect setting for this attractive pressed flower design. Fix a cluster of autumn plumbago leaves at one end of the oval card (supplied with the tray) and at the other end fix a smaller cluster of plumbago and autumn wild strawberry leaves. Now enlarge these two clusters with leaf sprays of *Acaena* 'Blue Haze'.

Keep each cluster fairly oval in shape. Working first on the smaller cluster, create a focal point with a red-tinged green hydrangea flower sitting on top of a wild carrot head. Now form a gentle curve of pink potentilla across the top and finish off with green hydrangea and red saxifrage. For the focal point of the larger cluster place a deep red potentilla on top of a head of wild carrot.

To add depth, tuck some pink potentilla and red-tinged hydrangea under the carrot head. Now place two smaller 'Red Ace' potentillas above the focal point. Make a gentle diagonal curve into the centre of the design with buds of Japanese crab apple and finish off with sprays of greyhair grass. Re-assemble the tray according to the manufacturer's instructions.

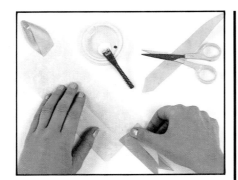

Blue delphiniums and pink candytuft are combined with mauve satin ribbon to create this most attractive pressed flower bookmark. Select a piece of grey imitation parchment paper and cut a rectangle 20cm x 8cm (8in x 3¼in). Crease and fold it in half lengthways. Open up the folded parchment and on the right hand page fix a loop of 2.5cm (1in) wide pale mauve ribbon, using latex adhesive. Cut two pieces of ribbon 9cm (3½in) long and trim in a V-shape. Fix these to the foot of the card as shown. Turn the card over to form the design on the page opposite that bearing the ribbons.

Begin with silverweed leaves facing alternately up the page. Next fix a blue delphinium near the base and overlap with mauve candytuft. Tuck in single candytuft florets under the leaves, gradually decreasing their size up the page and finishing with a few buds. Glue the two pages of card together. Cover both sides with matt protective film (cut to the height of the bookmark and twice the width).

Decorate an enamel canister with pressed flowers for an unusual gift. Secure the canister to your work surface with adhesive putty. Now take a large head of mauve candytuft and fix to the centre of the canister with latex adhesive. Surround the flower with salad burnet leaves and add two more candytuft flowers on either side. Paint over the design with 'two pack' varnish.

For the canister lid, coat with varnish before positioning a circle of salad burnet leaves – slightly apart – around the knob. Fill in between the leaves with large, single candytuft flowers. When dry, seal this design with two thin coats of varnish, feathering the edges with a lint-free cloth.

G ive your gift a period touch with this classic decoration. You can use a clear profile sketch or a photograph as a basis for your picture. Make a tracing of the outline and place it face down on the back of a piece of black paper. Redraw the design to transfer it.

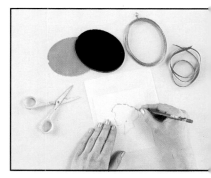

Cut out the motif with a pair of small, sharp scissors and glue the design to white paper. Trim the paper to fit your frame. Place the picture in the frame and glue a small ribbon bow to the top.

T o make these smart frames, cut two pieces of mounting board 25cm x 19cm (10in x 7½in). Cut a window 17cm x 11cm (7in x 4½in) in the centre of one piece. Cut two pieces of giftwrap to cover the frames. Lay the window mount on the wrong side of one piece and cut a window in the giftwrap, leaving a 2cm (¾in) margin. Snip to the corners and glue the margins down.

Cover the back of the frame with giftwrap, then cut two 1cm (⅜in) wide strips of mounting board 18cm (7¼in) long and one 22cm (8½in) long. Cover with paper and glue to the wrong side of the back just inside three of the edges. Spread glue on the strips and carefully place the front of the frame on top, checking that the outer edges are level.

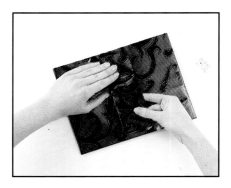

Cut a rectangle of mounting board 18cm x 6cm (7¼in x 2¼in) for the stand. Score across the stand 5cm (2in) from one end. Cover the stand with giftwrap and glue the scored end to the back with the other end level with either a long or short side depending on whether your photo is in landscape or portrait form. Bend the stand outwards.

Drop two or three colours onto the water and swirl together with the end of a paint brush. Cut plain paper to fit the tray. Wearing rubber gloves, start at one end of the tray and lower the paper onto the surface of the water so it can pick up the pattern. Carefully lift up the paper.

Leave the paper to dry overnight on newspaper. You can remove the paint from the tray by drawing strips of newspaper across the surface of the water.

Now you are ready to cover your gift. Cut a rectangle of marbled paper large enough to wrap around the book with a 2.5cm (1in) margin on all sides. Wrap the paper around the book, open the cover and glue the paper inside the opening edges.

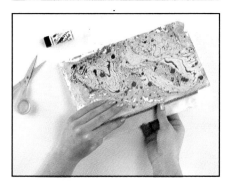

Prop up the book so the cover is open at a right angle. Snip the paper each side of the spine and stick the top and bottom margin inside the covers, folding under the corners.

For that extra special gift, cover a plain diary or note book in hand-marbled paper. Fill a shallow tray with water. Put spots of enamel paint on the water with a paint brush. If they sink the paint is too thick and needs thinning with a little white spirit. If they disperse into a faint film it is too thin and should be mixed with more paint.

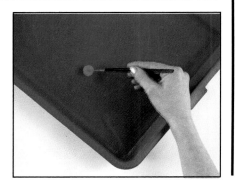

Push the paper at the ends of the spine between the spine and the pages with the points of a pair of scissors. Arrange jewellery stones on the cover and use a strong glue to stick them in place. Cut two pieces of paper to fit inside the covers and glue inside.

Use the traditional art of quilling to make this attractive gift box a gift in itself. Cut coloured paper strips 4mm (³/₁₆in) wide and about 20cm (8in) long. Scratch the end of a strip to soften the paper. Now coil the strip tightly between your thumb and finger. Release the coil so it springs open and glue the end against one side.

The coils can be gently squeezed into various shapes to fit your chosen design. Experiment with forming different shapes such as triangles and teardrops. To make smaller coils, cut shorter paper strips.

Draw a design on the lid of a wooden box and spread paper glue on a section of the lid. Arrange the coils on the glue and then move onto the next section. Fill in the whole design – any gaps around the motif can be filled with coils that match the colour of the box.

Transform ordinary pencils into these smart covered ones with scraps of wrapping paper. Choose round rather than hexagonal-shaped pencils. Cut a strip of wrapping paper wide enough to wrap around the pencil and as long as the pencil. Spray the back heavily with spray glue and wrap around the pencil.

To finish, simply trim away the excess at the end of the pencil with a pair of small scissors.

LETTER RACK

CLOCKWISE CARRIER BAG

There is no excuse for mislaying letters with this smart letter rack. From thick mounting board cut a rectangle 24cm x 8cm (9½in x 3¼in) for the front and 24cm x 10cm (9½in x 4in) for the back. Diagonally trim away the top corners and cover one side of each piece with giftwrap.

Cut giftwrap slightly smaller than the front and back sections and glue in position on the wrong side. Take a piece of wood 24cm (9½in) long by 3cm (1¼in) wide and 1cm (⅜in) thick. Cover the wood with coloured paper.

Cut a rectangle of mounting board 27cm x 7cm (10½in x 2¾in) for the base and cover with coloured paper. Use a strong glue to stick the front to one narrow edge of the wood keeping the lower edges level. Glue the back to the other side in the same way. Finish the letter rack by gluing this upper section centrally to the base.

Make this carrier bag and you have a gift bag for your presents or go a step further and make the bag itself the present. Cut a piece of thick yellow cardboard 57.5cm x 29cm (22⅝in x 11½in). Refer to the diagram on page 167 and score along the solid and broken lines. Cut away the lower right-hand corner and cut into the base along the solid lines.

Fold the bag forwards along the solid lines and backwards along the broken lines. Turn the bag over and, with a pencil, lightly divide the front into quarters. Cut out a small hole at the centre for the clockwork. Cut out four pieces of red paper 1.5cm x 1cm (⅝in x ⅜in) and glue on the divisions 7cm (2¾in) from the hole.

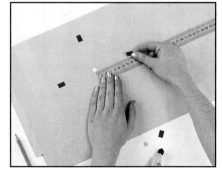

Rub out the pencil lines. Join the side seam by gluing the narrow tab under the opposite end. Fold under the small base sections then glue the long sections underneath. Cut two strips of green cardboard for handles 30cm x 1cm (12in x ⅜in). Glue the ends inside the top of the bag. Insert the clockwork rod through the hole and attach the hands.

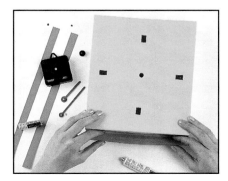

Paint a plain ceramic honey pot and transform it it into something striking for a unique gift. Using a fine paint brush and black ceramic paint, paint some bees on to the lid of the pot. If you are worried about painting free-hand, first draw the bees on with a chinagraph pencil. And if you are not even sure how to draw a bee, get a picture of one to copy.

Now paint the stripes with black ceramic paint. If, like this one, your pot is ridged, use the raised surface as a guide for your lines of paint. Otherwise you can use strips of masking tape to mask off those areas which are to be yellow. In order not to smudge the work, you may find it easier to paint the lower half first and then leave it to dry before painting the top half.

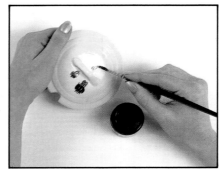

When all the black has dried, apply the yellow ceramic paint, carefully filling in the bee's striped body with a fine brush. Fill the pot with honey and have a nice breakfast!

Clowns are a very bright and jolly popular image and, painted on to wall plates like these, they make a colourful gift to decorate a child's room. Look at birthday cards, wrapping paper, toys and in children's books for inspiration.

Once you have drawn your design on paper, copy it on to a plate using a chinagraph pencil. When drawing your design, consider the shape of the plate; make the feet curl round the edge, as we have done here, and try to make the image fill as much of the plate as possible. Next, follow the chinagraph line with a line of black ceramic paint.

W̲ith a combination of ragging and flicking you can transform a plain china vase or jug into a work of art. You will need a piece of cloth for the ragging, a couple of fine artists' brushes and some ceramic paints. Dip the rag into one of the paints and then blot it onto some waste paper to remove any excess paint. Now begin to dab paint on to the vase.

Leave gaps between the dabs of paint to allow the background colour to show through. When you have evenly covered the surface, leave it to dry. Now spatter the vase with white ceramic paint, flicking the paint on with a fine brush. Once again, leave to dry.

Finally, apply some gold ceramic paint with a fine paint brush, forming clusters of little gold dots across the surface of the vase. Be sure to clean your brush thoroughly in turpentine when you have finished.

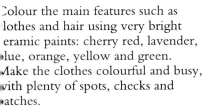

Colour the main features such as clothes and hair using very bright ceramic paints: cherry red, lavender, blue, orange, yellow and green. Make the clothes colourful and busy, with plenty of spots, checks and patches.

Finally, fill in the background with circles, triangles or wavy lines, painted in brightly contrasting colours. When the paint has dried, finish off with a protective coat of ceramic varnish.

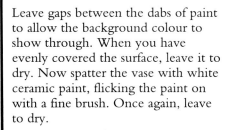

DECORATIVE DUCKS

M ade in the Phillipines from balsa wood, these lovely ornamental ducks are exported all over the world and are widely available in department stores. They are ideal for painting and make beautiful gifts. Draw your design on to the duck in pencil, either following one of the designs shown here or using a bird book as reference. Now start to paint.

Acrylic paints are ideal on this surface but you can also use glass or ceramic paints, or even a mixture of all three. Paint the main areas of colour first and then change to a finer brush and fill in details such as the eyes, the white ring round the neck and the markings on the wings and tail.

Finish off with a coat of polyurethane gloss varnish. If you have used a variety of paints remember that they will dry at different rates so make sure they are all dry before varnishing.

These jazzy potato printed cushions make inexpensive yet stylish gifts – you may even want to make some for your own home! Cut a potato in half and draw the design on to one half with a felt tip pen. Now cut around the motif so that the design stands proud of the background.

Paint some fabric paint on to the potato motif with a brush. Stamp off any excess paint on to some waste paper then print the motif on to your chosen fabric, leaving plenty of space for a second and even a third motif.

Cut another simple motif from the other half of the potato. Apply the colour as before and print on to the fabric. When the fabric has dried, iron on the back to fix the paints. Your fabric is now ready to be made up into cushions, curtains, blinds and so forth.

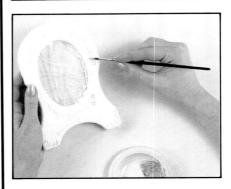

This pretty hand-painted frame is an ideal gift. Firstly, sand the frame until it is smooth and then give it a coat of white acrylic paint. Apply a second coat of paint if necessary and, when dry, draw the design with a soft pencil. Paint the design using acrylic paint in soft blues and greys with the flower centres in bright yellow.

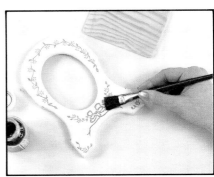

Remove the backing and the glass and give the frame a protective coat of polyurethane varnish.

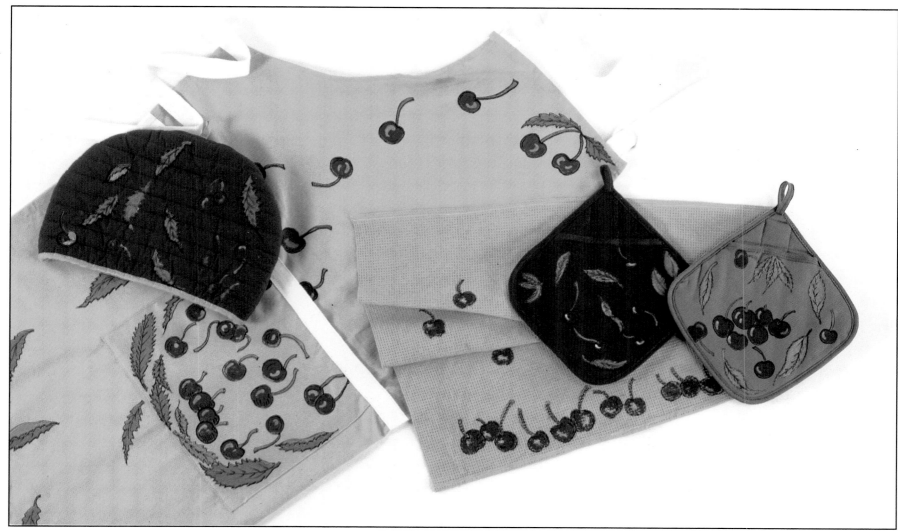

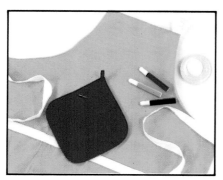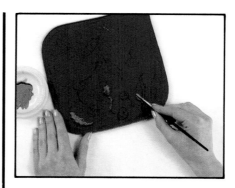

Decorate kitchen ware with a simple but effective design of cherries for a unique gift. You will need some fabric felt tip pens and/or some opaque fabric paint plus an apron, tea cosy, pot holder and tea towel to decorate.

Practise the design on some paper first, then, when you are confident, use a fine fabric felt tip pen to draw the outline of your design on to the fabric. Here, the leaves and cherries have been spaced out so that they appear to be tumbling down from the tree. On the apron pocket the leaves are grouped to act as a nest for the falling cherries.

Now fill in the outlines with red and green paint. On dark backgrounds you will need to use opaque paints; these are harder to apply than the felt tip pens, so be patient and keep going over the design to achieve the intensity of colour desired.

When the paint is dry, use the black felt tip pen to add veins to the leaves and shading to the cherries. To complete the design, add white highlights to the cherries. this can be done either with a pin or with the opaque fabric paint. Finally, iron the back of the fabric to fix the paints.

Open out the leg seams and sew the boot to the leg along E-D-E. Then fold the boot with right sides facing and sew the front to the side body along seam G-E on both sides, ensuring that point A matches. Sew seam E-F in black thread.

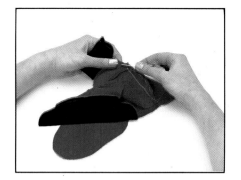

Close the back seam from G to C, leaving a gap for turning. Sew the boot soles into place. Turn the body the right way out and stuff firmly. Ladder stitch the back opening closed and place the body to one side.

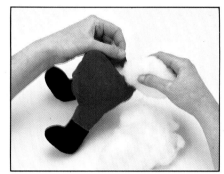

For the jacket, join the two halves together by sewing seam L-M-L. Sew the sleeves to the jacket along J-K-J, easing to fit. Sew a strip of white fur fabric 14cm x 4cm (5½in x 1½in) to the edge of the sleeves, keeping the right sides together. Fold the strip over the raw edge of the sleeve and sew down on the reverse side.

Fold the sleeves in half and sew up the side seam O-J-N on both sides. At the base of the jacket, sew a strip of white fur fabric 42cm x 4cm (16½in x 1½in). Fold the strip back over the raw edge of the jacket and sew into place on the reverse side.

MATERIALS

Red velvet or felt
Black felt
Pink or flesh coloured felt
Very long white fur fabric
Short white fur fabric, for
  pom pom
Ribbon
Filling

Delight the kids with this charming Santa doll. Size up the pattern overleaf and cut out all the pieces in the appropriate fabrics. For the body, sew the inside legs to the front body from A to B on either side. With right sides together, join the front body with attached legs to the side body from point D to C, matching point B. Repeat for the other side.

For the hood, turn up a narrow double hem on each short side. Sew a strip of white fur fabric 23cm x 4cm (9¼in x 1½in) to the front edge in the same way as for the jacket. Fold the hood in half and, with right sides together, sew seam P-Q.

Turn the hood the right way out and add a short piece of ribbon to each front corner of the hood. Fold down the point of the hood. Sew a running stitch around the edge of the pom pom and gather. Stuff gently, then pull the thread to gather tightly. Attach the pom pom to the side of the hood.

Place the pairs of arms right sides together and sew all around, leaving the top straight edges open. Turn and stuff the arms, then oversew arms to the body sides. Place the jacket on the body.

To make the head, sew up the darts on both head pieces. Place the two halves together with right sides facing and sew around the head, leaving the bottom straight edge open.

Turn the head the right way out. Place some filling into the head, stuffing it firmly. Gather the bottom edge of the head with a running stitch, then ladder stitch the head to the body.

Using a running stitch, gather the edge of the nose. Place a small amount of filling in the centre, then fasten off securely. Stitch the nose to the centre of the face. Cut two eye circles out of black felt and sew them into position above the nose.

Fold the side flaps of the long white hair piece down and sew seam R-S on either side. Sew the beard to the front of the hair piece from T to U on both sides. Turn the right way out and pull onto Santa's head so that the top of the beard just touches the nose. Stitch into place. Put the hood on Santa's head and tie into place under the beard.

One square represents 2.5cm (1in)

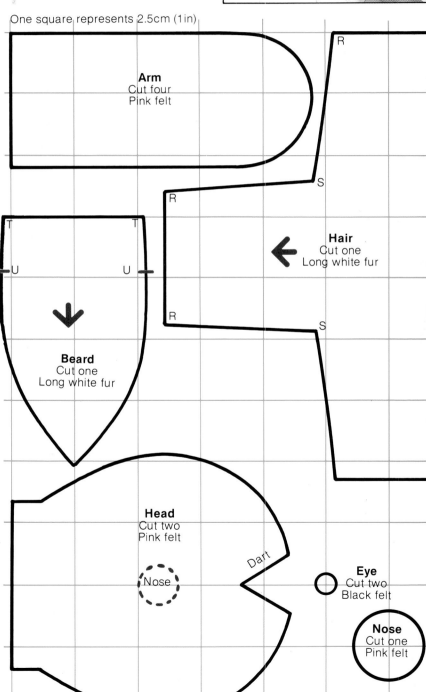

Arm
Cut four
Pink felt

Hair
Cut one
Long white fur

Beard
Cut one
Long white fur

Head
Cut two
Pink felt

Nose

Dart

Eye
Cut two
Black felt

Nose
Cut one
Pink felt

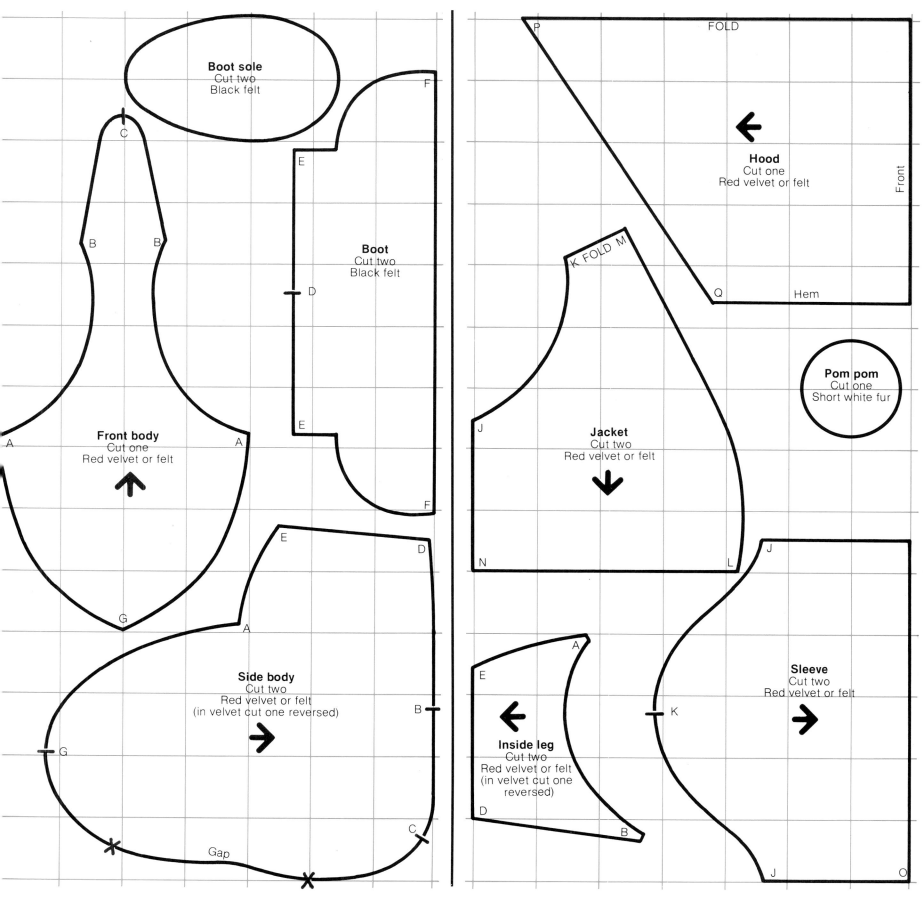

Boot sole
Cut two
Black felt

F

E

Boot
Cut two
Black felt

C

B B

D

E

Front body
Cut one
Red velvet or felt

A A

E

F

G

E D

A

Side body
Cut two
Red velvet or felt
(in velvet cut one reversed)

B

G

C

Gap

X X

P FOLD

←

Hood
Cut one
Red velvet or felt

Front

K FOLD M

Q Hem

Pom pom
Cut one
Short white fur

J

Jacket
Cut two
Red velvet or felt

↓

N L J

A

E

←

Inside leg
Cut two
Red velvet or felt
(in velvet cut one reversed)

D

B

K

Sleeve
Cut two
Red velvet or felt

→

J O

Pierce tiny holes in the eye positions and turn the head the right way out. Insert the safety eyes in the holes and secure on the reverse with metal washers. Stuff the head, shaping it into a round fat ball. Using a running stitch, gather the raw edge at the base and finish off securely.

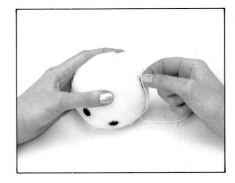

Fold the nose piece in half and sew along the straight edge. Turn the right way out and stuff firmly. Gather the raw edge of the nose and finish off. Place this end on head at a central position between the eyes and ladder stitch firmly into place. Using black embroidery thread, stitch a 'V'-shaped mouth below the eyes. Then ladder stitch the head to the body.

Place each pair of arms right sides together and sew all around, leaving the top straight edges open. Turn the arms the right way out and stuff them, adding far less filling to the top halves. Turn the raw edges in and oversew the arms into position on either side of the neck. Secure the hands to the body with a couple of stitches.

MATERIALS

Short pile white fur fabric
Black, red and green felt
Scrap of orange felt for nose
1 pair 13.5mm black safety
*   eyes with metal washers*
Black embroidery thread
Filling

Sew the two hat brim pieces together around both the outer and inner edges. Fold the main body of the hat in half and sew around the short edge. Place the completed cylinder on top of the hat brim in a central position and oversew the two pieces together around the inner circle. Oversew the hat top into position and put some filling inside the hat.

Size up the pattern opposite and cut out all the pieces in the appropriate fabrics. Make up the body using the same method as for Santa's body (see page 155). Stuff the body well, making it fat and rounded. Sew the dart on each of the head pieces. Then place the two halves right sides together and sew around the head, leaving the bottom straight edge open.

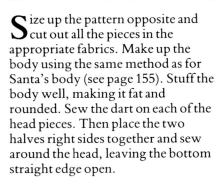

Put the hat on the head in a lopsided position and stitch down. Wrap a red felt strip 19cm x 2cm (7½in x ¾in) around the base of the hat. Overlap ends and sew into place. Sew holly leaves onto the hat and buttons onto the body. Cut a red or green felt strip 5cm x 40cm (2in x 16in). Fringe the ends and tie scarf around the snowman's neck.

One square represents 2.5cm (1in)

Hat brim
Cut two
Black felt

Hat top
Cut one
Black felt

Hat
Cut one
Black felt

Nose
Cut one
Orange felt

Button
Cut three
Black felt

G

Front body
Cut one
White fur

A   A

Arm
Cut four
White fur

Head
Cut two
White fur

Eye

Dart

Nose

Eye

Holly
Cut two
Green felt

B   B

Boot
Cut two
Black felt

E

F

D

F

E

Boot sole
Cut two
Black felt

C

E   D

A

Side body
Cut two (one reversed)
White fur

B

B

Inside leg
Cut two (one reversed)
White fur

A

G

C

E   D

Gap

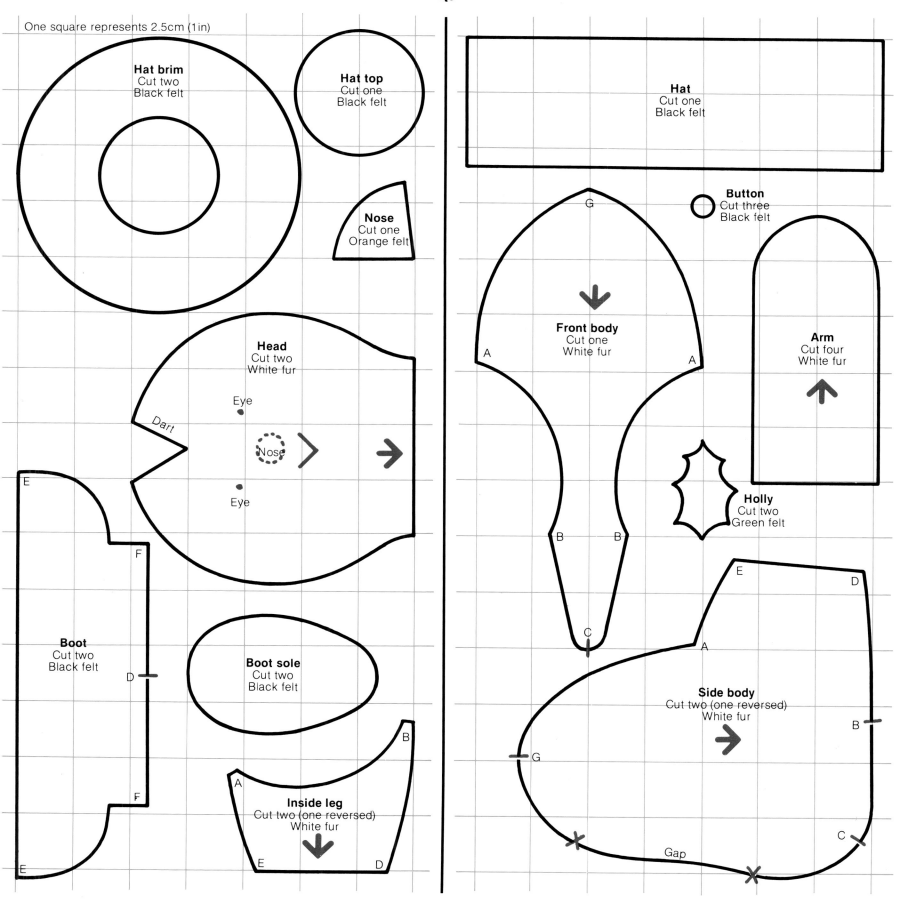

Join the head gusset piece to the side of the head on the side body piece by sewing seam J-K. Repeat on other side. Then sew up seam J-D at the front of the head.

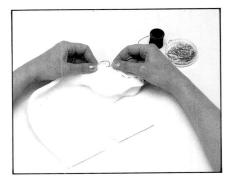

Sew the inside body to the side body, starting at seam D-E. Then sew seam F-G and finally seam H-B. Repeat on other side.

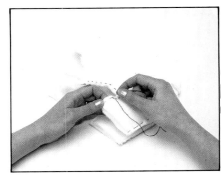

MATERIALS

30cm (12in) white fur fabric
1 pair 13.5mm black safety
  eyes with metal washers
1 small plastic nose
Black embroidery thread
Filling

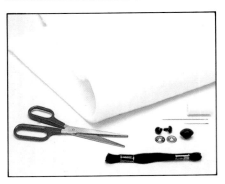

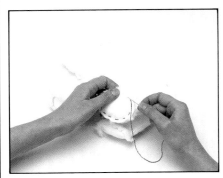

Fold the tail in half lengthwise. Sew along the curved edge, leaving the top open. Turn the tail, poking out the tip carefully. Sew seam K-B on the back of the bear, sewing in the tail at the same time where the two darts meet. Open out and stretch the bottoms of the feet and sew in the foot pads.

This charming toy will delight any child. Size up the pattern opposite and cut out all the pieces. Pierce a tiny hole at the eye position and cut a slit for the ears on each side body piece. Join both pieces of the inside body by sewing seam A-B, leaving a gap for turning and filling. Open out the inside body. Sew the under chin piece to the inside body along seam C-A-C.

Turn the bear the right way out. Insert the safety eyes through the holes made earlier and secure on the reverse with metal washers. Poke a tiny hole at the very end of the snout and secure the plastic nose in the same way.

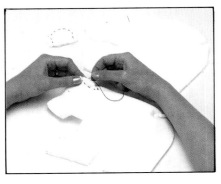

Sew up the darts at the rear of the side body pieces. Sew both halves of ears together, leaving the straight edge open. Turn the right way out and make a small tuck at the raw edge of the ear on both sides to curve the ear slightly inwards and oversew into place. Push the straight edge through the slit in the side body and sew the ears into position through all layers of fabric.

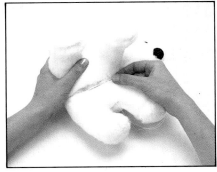

Fill the bear with stuffing, starting at the feet. Flatten the feet slightly as the filling is added. Mould the head shape by pushing more filling into the cheeks. When satisfied with the general shape of the bear, close the gap in the tummy using a ladder stitch.

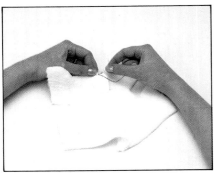

With black embroidery thread, stitch through the feet four times on each paw to form claws. Using the same thread, embroider a smile on the bear's face. Finish off the mouth on either side with a small stitch at right angles to the main stitch.

Finally, taking a long needle and white thread, pull the eyes slightly together by passing the threaded needle from corner to corner of the opposite eyes, through the head. Fasten off securely.

One square represents 2.5cm (1in)

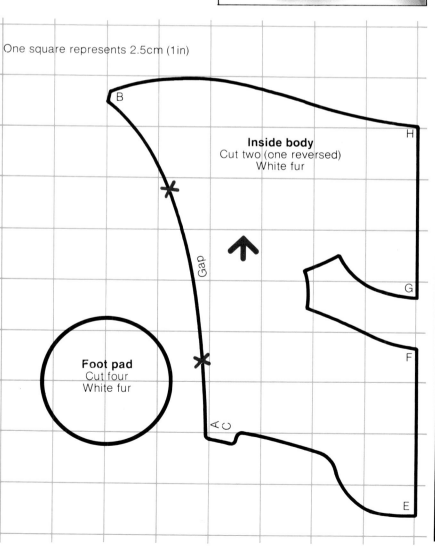

Inside body
Cut two (one reversed)
White fur

Foot pad
Cut four
White fur

B

H

Gap

A
C

E

G

F

J

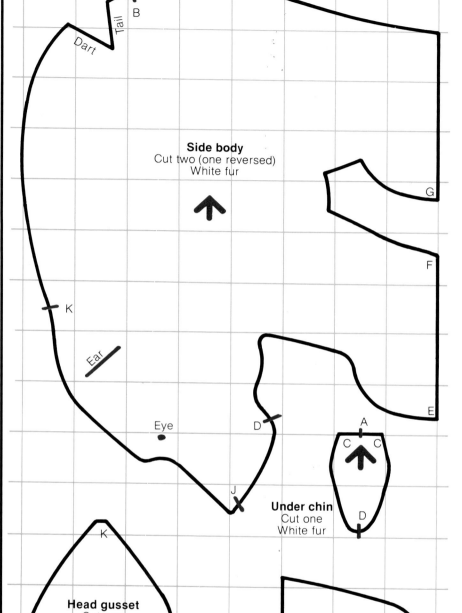

Side body
Cut two (one reversed)
White fur

Dart

Tail

B

G

F

E

K

Ear

Eye

D

J

Under chin
Cut one
White fur

A

C   C

D

Head gusset
Cut one
White fur

K

J

Tail
Cut one
White fur

Ear
Cut four
White fur

Size up the templates on the following pages as follows: draw up a grid of 2.5cm (1in) squares, then copy the design onto your grid, square by square, using the grid lines as a guide.

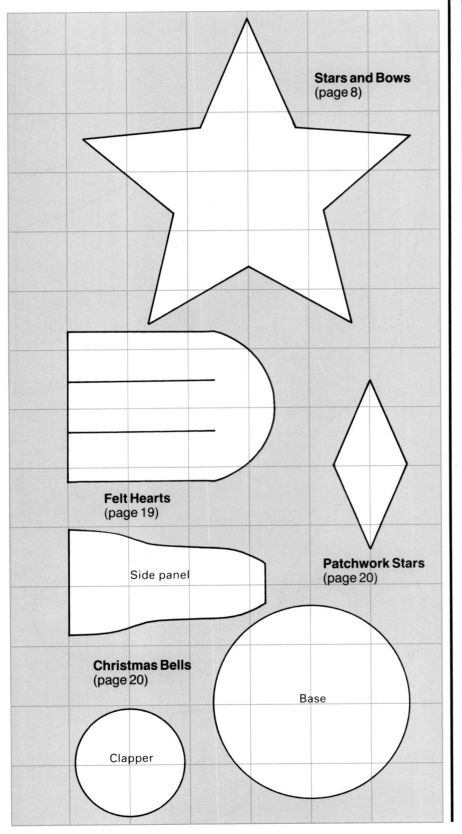

Stars and Bows
(page 8)

Felt Hearts
(page 19)

Side panel

Patchwork Stars
(page 20)

Christmas Bells
(page 20)

Clapper

Base

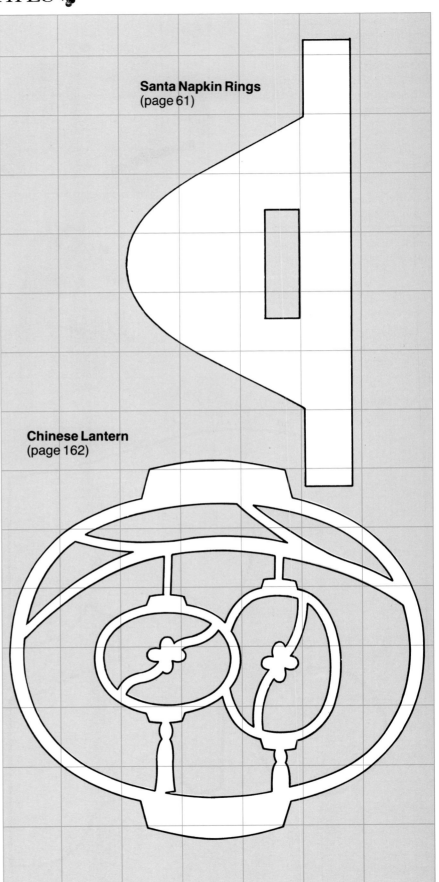

Santa Napkin Rings
(page 61)

Chinese Lantern
(page 162)

Star Garland
(page 29)

**Christmas Tree
Frieze**
(page 29)

Incognito
(page 64)

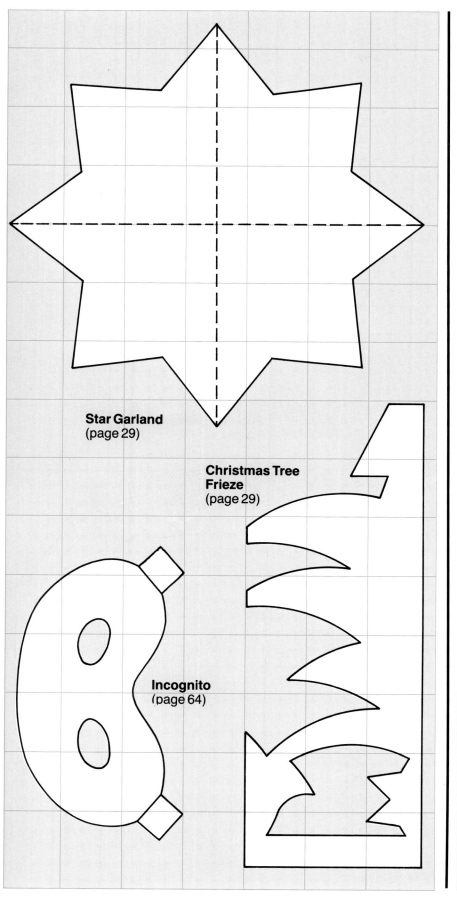

Strike Up the Band
(page 65)

Place on fold

Dancing Santas
(page 27)

Masquerade
(page 47)

Place on fold

Candy Sleigh
(page 51)

Blue Angel
(page 17)

Place on fold

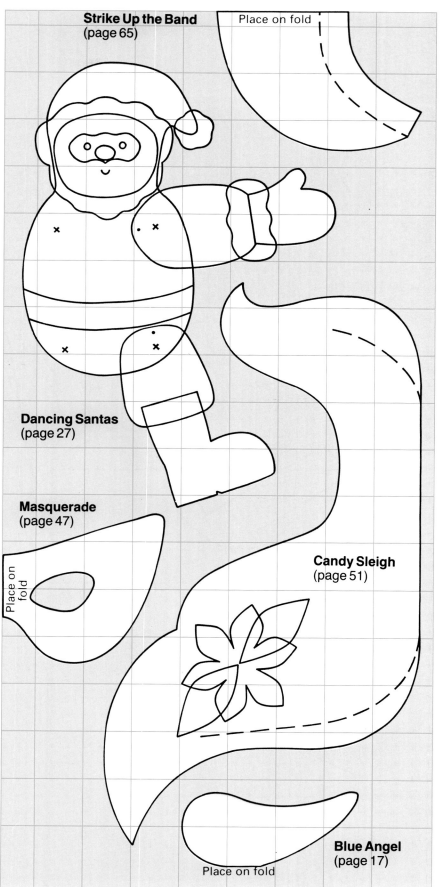

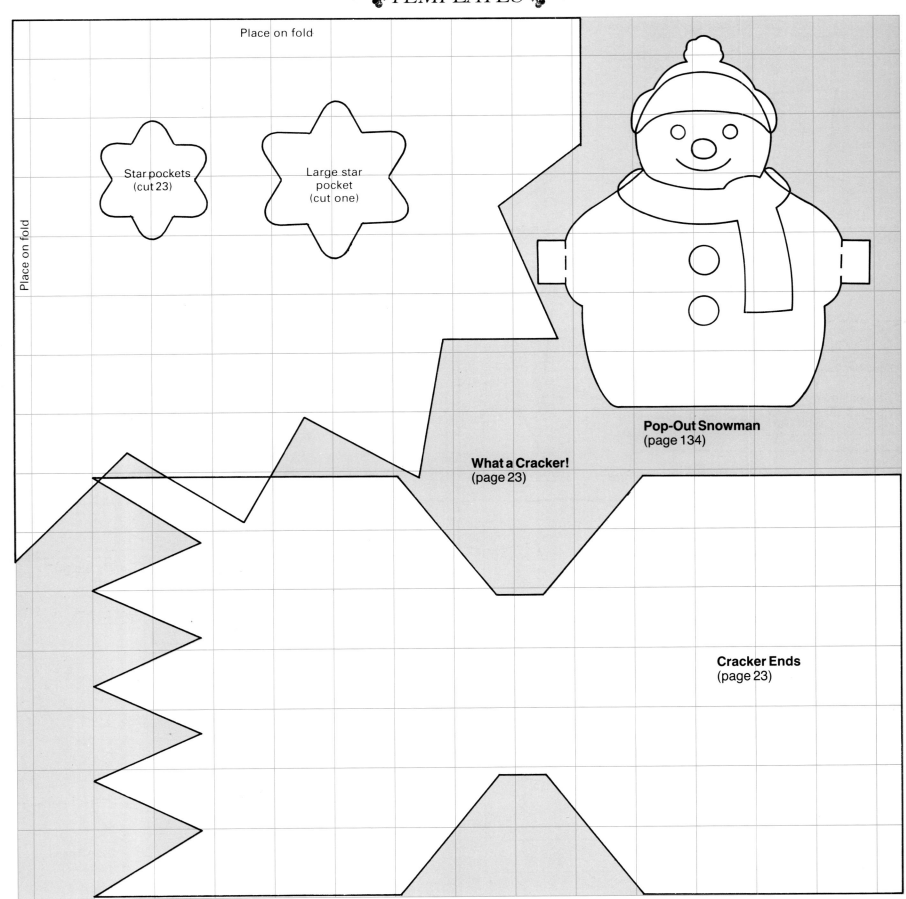

Place on fold

Place on fold

Star pockets
(cut 23)

Large star
pocket
(cut one)

Pop-Out Snowman
(page 134)

What a Cracker!
(page 23)

Cracker Ends
(page 23)

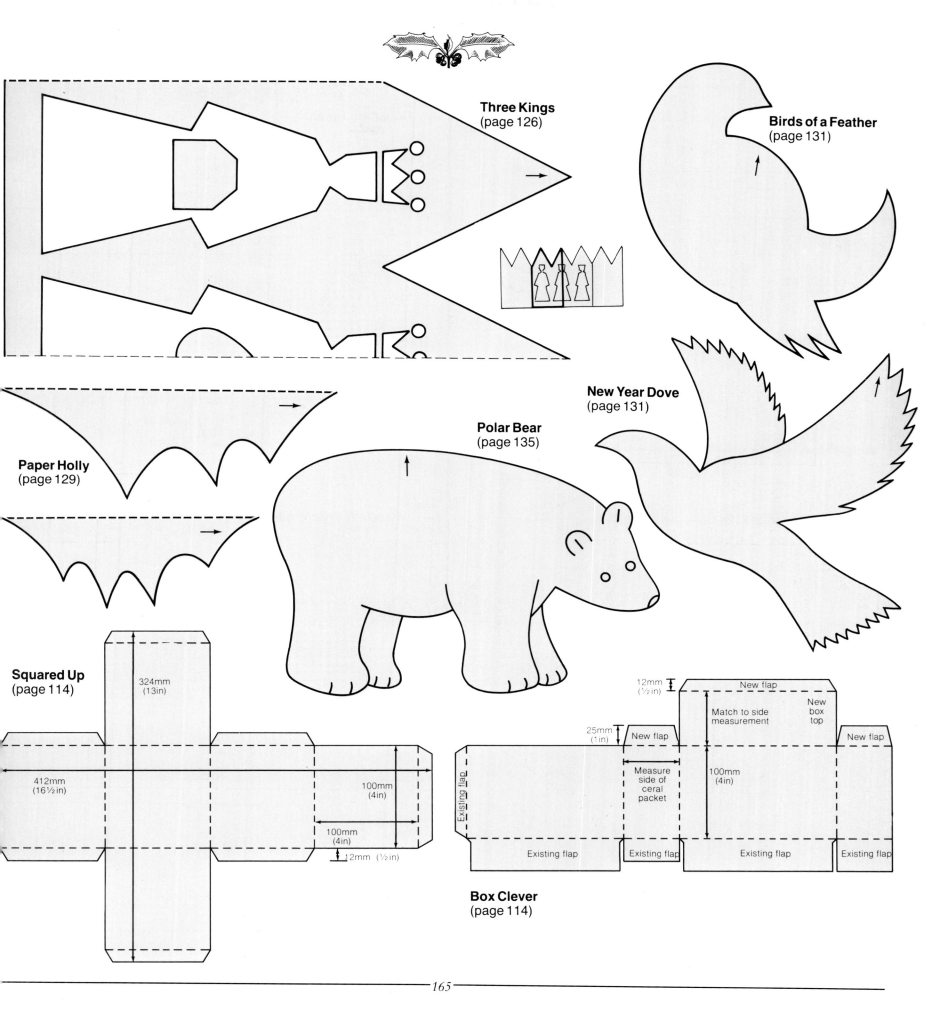

Three Kings
(page 126)

Birds of a Feather
(page 131)

New Year Dove
(page 131)

Paper Holly
(page 129)

Polar Bear
(page 135)

Squared Up
(page 114)

324mm
(13in)

412mm
(16½in)

100mm
(4in)

100mm
(4in)

12mm (½in)

12mm
(½in)

New flap

New
box
top

Match to side
measurement

25mm
(1in)

New flap

New flap

New flap

Existing flap

Measure
side of
ceral
packet

100mm
(4in)

Existing flap

Existing flap

Existing flap

Existing flap

Box Clever
(page 114)

Smart Sachets (page 110)

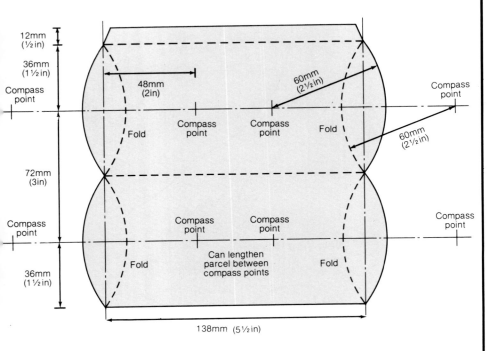

12mm (½in)

36mm (1½in)

Compass point

48mm (2in)

60mm (2½in)

Compass point

Compass point

Fold

Fold

60mm (2½in)

Compass point

72mm (3in)

Compass point

Compass point

Compass point

Compass point

Fold

Fold

Can lengthen parcel between compass points

36mm (1½in)

Fold

Fold

138mm (5½in)

Boxed In (page 85)

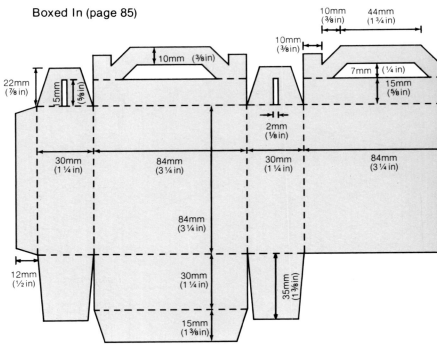

10mm (⅜in)

44mm (1¾in)

10mm (⅜in)

10mm (⅜in)

7mm (¼in)

22mm (⅞in)

15mm (⅝in)

15mm (⅝in)

2mm (⅛in)

30mm (1¼in)

84mm (3¼in)

30mm (1¼in)

84mm (3¼in)

84mm (3¼in)

12mm (½in)

30mm (1¼in)

35mm (1⅜in)

15mm (1⅜in)

The Pyramids (page 112)

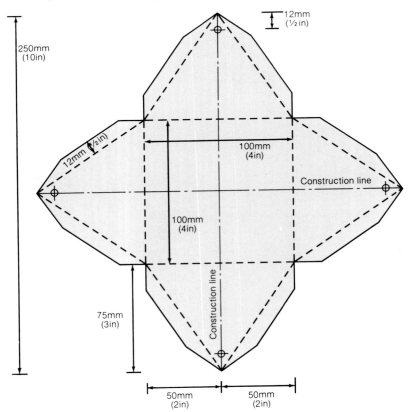

250mm (10in)

12mm (½in)

12mm (½in)

100mm (4in)

Construction line

100mm (4in)

Construction line

75mm (3in)

50mm (2in)

50mm (2in)

Handle With Care! (page 113)

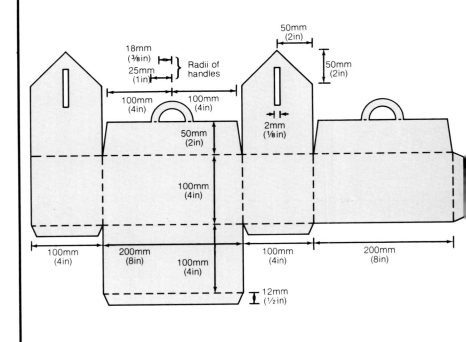

18mm (⅜in)

50mm (2in)

25mm (1in)

Radii of handles

50mm (2in)

100mm (4in)

100mm (4in)

2mm (⅛in)

50mm (2in)

100mm (4in)

100mm (4in)

200mm (8in)

100mm (4in)

200mm (8in)

100mm (4in)

12mm (½in)

SCIENTIFIC CLASSIFICATION

The following is an alphabetical list of the common names of plants
used in this book and their Latin equivalents

Common name	Latin name	Common name	Latin name
Baby's breath	*Gypsophila paniculata*	Oak	*Quercus*
Bottlebrush	*Callistemon*	Pearl everlasting	*Anaphalis*
Carnation	*Dianthus*	Poppy	*Papaver*
Chinese lantern	*Physalis*	Rhodanthe (sunray)	*Rhodanthe manglesii =*
Clubrush	*Scirpus*		*Helipterum manglesii*
Cypress	*Cupressus*	Rabbit's or hare's	*Lagarus ovatus*
Glixia (grass daisy)	*Aphyllanthes*	tail grass	
	monspeliensis	Rose	*Rosa*
Holly	*Ilex aquifolium*	Safflower	*Carthamus tinctorius*
Honesty	*Lunaria annua*	Sandflower	*Ammobium alatum*
(silver dollar plant)		Sea lavender	*Limonium tataricum*
Ivy	*Hedera*	September flower	*Aster ericoides*
Larkspur	*Delphinium consolida*	Spruce	*Picea*
Lavender	*Lavandula angustifolia*	Statice	*Limonium sinuatum*
Lily	*Lilium*	Strawflower	*Helichrysum*
Love-lies-bleeding	*Amaranthus caudatus*	(or everlasting)	
Nipplewort (Dutch	*Laspana communis*	Sunray	*Helipterum*
exporters call it broom bloom)		Yarrow	*Achillea*

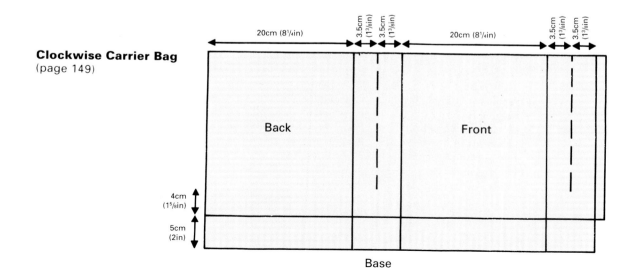

Clockwise Carrier Bag
(page 149)

20cm (8¼in)   3.5cm (1⅜in)   3.5cm (1⅜in)   20cm (8¼in)   3.5cm (1⅜in)   3.5cm (1⅜in)

Back

Front

4cm (1⅝in)

5cm (2in)

Base

INDEX